Yusuf and Zuleika

The Return of the Despot

Murzban Jal

AAKAR

Yusuf and Zuleika: The Return of the Despot
Murzban Jal

First Published 2019

ISBN 978-93-5002-599-4

Published by
AAKAR BOOKS
28 E Pocket IV, Mayur Vihar Phase I
Delhi 110 091 India
aakarbooks@gmail.com

Laser Typeset at
Sakshi Computers, Delhi

Printed at
D.K. Fine Art Press, Delhi

Contents

Acknowledgements

In celebration of the centenary year of the Bolshevik Revolution, Anjiah Nanapaneni from the Centre for Scientific Socialism, Acharya Nagarjuna University invited me to deliver a lecture. The first thought that occurred to me was on the question of secularism in Asian societies and the need for a Marxist idea of secularism that is rigorously different from the liberal one. I dropped the idea and in contextualizing the Bolshevik Revolution I thought how my then recently published book *Challenges for the Indian Left*, especially on the part of the Stalinist counterrevolution could form the main part of my lecture. The lecture had to come out in the form of a book. And in writing on the margins of the victorious counterrevolution I thought that dramaturgy could best tackle the spectacles of hyper-capitalism (that boasts that it is the best society, in fact even society that marks the "end of history") as well as the horrible phantasmagoria of the Stalinist counterrevolution. It is then that the idea of Yusuf and Zuleika arose.

I would like to thank Anjiah Nanapaneni, the Indian Institute of Education, Pune, the social science research institute started by the legendary educationist J.P. Naik, the Indian Council of Social Scientific Research, New Delhi, as well as Jyoti Bawane, Surinder Jodhka, Surendra Jondhale, Deepak Gaikwad, Satybhama Kharat and Mangal Deokule, just as I curse all the counterrevolutionaries and enemies of knowledge and love.

The Word

Jalāl ad-Dīn Muhammad Rumi

Zuleika had a secret, every word
or phrase she spoke in secret ways referred

to her beloved Yusuf. If she said,
"The moon is out tonight," she meant instead

to say she loved him. When she said, "Aloe"
or "spice" or "bread," her confidantes would know

that it was code for Yusuf; every phrase
a tribute to his beauty and his ways.

You could say, and by now you may have guessed,
that Zuleika lived a life that was obsessed

with Yusuf; she had turned the very gift
of speech to magic, making meanings drift

and making words say what they never meant.
The blandest phrases turned to sentiment

and thoughts and praises of Yusuf. When she cursed
aloud she meant she wanted time reversed

to once again the hour they last met
when parting made her words turn to regret.

His was the name that every morning burst
from her lips and quenched her every thirst

his name would warm Zuleika in the cold.
And just so, all believers should be told,

that when you seek salvation for your soul
you merge into the ocean of the whole

so lover and beloved are the same
your Zuleika is merely Yusuf's name

and even though your linguist thinks it odd
all pronouncements are one–the word is "God."

The syllable that permeates all things
exploding stars and songs the robin sings.

* * *

1
Prelude: The Temptations of Yusuf and Zuleika

To produce a new "improved version" of humanity—this is the future of communism.

Leon Trotsky

Yusuf, in actuality, besides being the Hebrew slave soon to become Prophet in the Judaic tradition who reappears in Islamic literature, also appears as Iosif Dzhugashvili, or Josef Stalin, as history would know him. While there are a number of Yusufs or Josefs, there are two who are diametrically opposite—the first is the revolutionary messianic rendering of Yusuf-Josef, a rendering that is celebrated in Islamic Sufi literature as the celebration of universal love, and the second is of the counterrevolutionary par excellence, Josef Stalin.

To understand the first Yusuf-Josef let us go to the first book in the *Torah*, the 'Book of Genesis'. This is how he appears in the *Torah*. It must be noted that there are three characters in the plot mentioned below: the Hebrew slave Yusuf or Josef (who is also an interpreter of dreams), his Egyptian master Potiphar and Potiphar's wife Zuleika. Josef is a handsome man and Zuleika falls in love with him, trying to covert with him. Josef as the faithful slave of his master Potiphar resists Zuleika's temptations. Zuleika is enraged:

> Potiphar left everything he had in Joseph's care; with Joseph in charge, he did not concern himself with anything except the

> food he ate. Now Joseph was well-built and handsome, and after a while his master's wife took notice of Joseph and said, "Come to bed with me!" But he refused. "With me in charge," he told her, "my master does not concern himself with anything in the house; everything he owns he has entrusted to my care. No one is greater in this house than I am. My master has withheld nothing from me except you, because you are his wife. How then could I do such a wicked thing and sin against God?" And though she spoke to Joseph day after day, he refused to go to bed with her or even be with her. One day he went into the house to attend to his duties, and none of the household servants was inside. She caught him by his cloak and said, "Come to bed with me!" But he left his cloak in her hand and ran out of the house. When she saw that he had left his cloak in her hand and had run out of the house, she called her household servants. "Look," she said to them, "this Hebrew has been brought to us to make sport of us! He came in here to sleep with me, but I screamed. When he heard me scream for help, he left his cloak beside me and ran out of the house." She kept his cloak beside her until his master came home. Then she told him this story: "That Hebrew slave you brought us came to me to make sport of me. But as soon as I screamed for help, he left his cloak beside me and ran out of the house." When his master heard the story his wife told him, saying, "This is how your slave treated me," he burned with anger. Joseph's master took him and put him in prison, the place where the king's prisoners were confined.[1]

Though the *Torah* does not mention the name of this "wife" that is "seduced" accordingly to her phantasmagorical imagination, she appears as Zuleika in later Islamic literature. And as Zuleika she is immortalized in the poetry of Rumi, Hafiz and Goethe. While the *Torah* and the *Koran* do not explicitly mention the deep layer of this narrative, it must be mentioned that Potiphar dies while Zuleika ages. One day as Yusuf is walking past, she hears people crying "Yusuf! Yusuf!" and rushes to greet her old love. Strangely Yusuf has not aged while she has. Yusuf then recognizes her and hugs her, whereby she becomes young and beautiful once again.

In this narrative, Yusuf is no puritan. He is desirous, just as Zuleika is. At this moment one needs to intervene. For the *Torah* may not exactly be a story of love. In fact it could be of the establishment of patriarchy. After all, the Judaic god, Jehovah, is male, is angry and on the slightest pretext vents his anger on his creation. In my *The Seductions of Karl Marx* I put this patriarchal narrative central and said that a subversion of this entire male-centric narrative is necessary for human emancipation to take place.

And it is here that I recall Erich Fromm who talks of how the *Torah* "as the primary text of Jewish monotheism represents a male victory over the female deities, over the matriarchal remnants in the social structure."[2] After all, in the Judaic myth of creat.on it is the male god who speaks and in this speech-act creation takes place. Jehovah literally has robbed the female principle of her natural rights to procreate. It has also robbed the very act of love. The myth signifies the primal castration anxiety. Love, literally, becomes the Original Sin. And Western civilization since then has been grappling and struggling with this unbearable load over its head.

In contrast is the Yusuf-Zuleika love which we keep central to this work. Both are filled with desire and passion and both celebrate this very desire and passion. In Goethe's *West-East Divan* we have the following verse where Zuleika says:

> In mirrors, beautiful am I.
> But fate will make me age, you say.
> Unchanging, we—in Allah's eye:
> Love him in me—right now. Today.[3]

and

> That a Josef Zuleika delighted
> Required no art;
> He was young; youth draws the heart.
> He was handsome, had a true attraction—
> She had beauty; mutual reaction. But that you, for whom I have waited so long,
> Send fiery, youthful love-looks bright,
> And love me now, and will later delight—
> That's what my songs are made to praise,
> And I'll call you "Zuleika" all my days.[4]

Yusuf and Zuleika is thus a tale of eternal love. It is about revolution and counterrevolution. It is also about betrayal. Note

Goethe's verse below that Marx loved quoting. Note the words "torture" and "torment" along with the word "pleasure".

> Should this torture then torment us
> Since it brings us greater pleasure?
> Were not through the rule of Timur
> Souls devoured without measure? [5]

While the two words ("torture" and "torment") are by and large, especially in Marx's rendering in his celebrated essay 'The British Rule in India', related to the torture and torment of colonialism which Marx compares with the massacre and ransacking of Delhi by Timur in 1398, while "pleasure" is allegedly of the so-called "progress" that colonial-capitalism would bring with the destruction of Caste Oligarchy; there is another rendering. In this rendering the torture and torment is of unquenched love, love that is always suspended.

I am keeping this verse central to this small book. Both the renderings are also central to this work—that of love and that of massacre. This is how the Yusuf-Zuleika tale unfolds. The first Yusuf-Josef is the lover and messiah, not to forget the interpreter of dreams both in the *Torah* and the *Koran*. The second is Josef Stalin—the pretender messiah—who appears as Timur. Thus the first rendering of Yusuf and Zuleika is of Marx's love for humanity that he draws in the *Economic and Philosophic Manuscripts of 1844* and *Capital*. It is philosophical. The second is of the terrible consequences of the failure of the Bolshevik Revolution in not spreading to other parts of the world in the 1920s. It is in this failure that Stalin appears on the scene of history. Stalin is the perfection of the figure of Yusuf who ignores Zuleika's love. But he is not merely Yusuf II. He is also Timur.

There are thus two Yusufs (within the first Yusuf, the messianic Yusuf or Yusuf I), one that apparently ignores Zuleika's love. This is the Yusuf who appears on the surface reading of Genesis 39 of the *Torah* and Sura 12 in the *Koran*. But there is also a secret Yusuf which later Persian poets understood only too well. This Yusuf does not ignore Zuleika.

Regarding Zuleika there is no confusion. For Marx, Zuleika is love immortal in the form of the working class and the Revolution. For Stalin, Zuleika is Trotsky. For Marx, Zuleika has to be loved.

For Stalin, Zuleika has to be killed. *Yusuf and Zuleika* is about love, love triumphant and love betrayed.

In essence this little book is a celebration of the centenary of the Bolshevik Revolution. Basically it is a philosophical outline of my book *Challenges for the Indian Left* that I penned with the loving aide of several scholar-comrades. It is thus a reflection on this entire book keeping the focus on my introduction, 'In the Name of Marx' which now has come out as a separate book[6]. Unlike other Marxist scholars, who in the name of libertarianism, renounced and denounced the Bolshevik Revolution, this work is in defence of the Revolution. We thus have to love the Revolution, just as we have to love Yusuf and Zuleika. However in this love for the Revolution and unlike uncritical historiography that has seen a smooth transition from Lenin to Stalin, this work keeps the figure of Stalin as the counterrevolutionary par excellence and the betrayer of Marxism-Leninism. Stalin as Yusuf II betrays Zuleika, not once (as it appears in the *Torah*) but twice.

And to this betrayal there is a deeper logic that is needed to explain the Stalin phenomena and why the Gulags replaced Marx's idea of human emancipation. Stalin is not merely Yusuf II. He is not only Timur but also Genghis Khan. Note Marx here, to understand how the ghost of Genghis Khan would hover in Russia even after the Bolshevik Revolution:

> Thus, the Russia of the Normans completely disappears from the stage, and the few weak reminiscences in which it still outlived itself, dissolves before the terrible apparition of Genghis Khan. The bloody mire of Mongolian slavery, not the rude glory of the Norman epoch, forms the cradle of Muscovy, and modern Russia is but a metamorphosis of Muscovy.[7]

Further in the same work, Marx says:

> It is the terrible and abject school of Mongolian slavery that Muscovy was nursed and grew up. It gathered strength only by becoming a virtuoso in the craft of serfdom. Even when emancipated, Muscovy continued to perform its traditional part of the slave as master. At length Peter the Great coupled the political craft of the Mongol slave with the proud aspiration of the Mongol master, to whom Genghis Khan had, by will, bequeathed his conquest of the earth.[8]

Consequently this work claims that it was not Marx and Marxism that spoke after the death of Lenin, not even the ghost of Marx, but that of Genghis Khan. I have also said that Stalin was dressed as Marx and Stalinism dressed as Marxism, but underneath this fake dress was the reality of the counterrevolutionary and barbarian Genghis Khan.

If however this Great Khan is what Stalin modelled himself after, probably the figure of Louis Bonaparte also fits in to describe Stalin. In *The Eighteenth Brumaire of Louis Bonaparte* Marx had talked of Louis Bonaparte as the prince of the lumpen proletariat and also talked of the state that he (Bonaparte) created seeming to soar above all classes. Nicos Poulantzas called this the "exceptional capitalist state". Not much has been written of this Stalinist counterrevolution and this "exceptional capitalist state" where a brutal form of Orientalist despotic state capitalism was created, a state capitalism that was made to soar above all classes. Not much has been written on the alternative to capitalism, probably with the exception of Peter Hudis's *Marx's Concept of the Alternative to Capitalism*.[9]

This little book intends to be scholarly in the very Marxist sense. Thus just as Lenin had said in his *State and Revolution* that detailed quotes would be made from Marx and Engels to explain his (Lenin's) point of view, I have also tried to engage in a form of revolutionary scholarly theory. But the "scholarly" sense of this monograph is not scholastic and esoteric. It is intended for grassroots comrades to read and understand.

We all know that there is a strong sense of aesthetics in Marxism and one has to understand revolution (as Lenin had informed us) as an *art form*. Marx never wrote dry treatises. Instead there was a sense of aesthetics in his works where the creation of the Revolutionary Sublime surrounded all his works. *Capital* was thus not merely a work in the critique of political economy, but a symphony, in fact even an opera. After the one hundred and fiftieth anniversary of *Capital*, Vol. I and in the year that celebrates Marx's two hundred Birth Anniversary we also remember this great work. In this remembrance we note how its melodies ought to be played out throughout the world.

Yusuf II or the Stalin Question

One may say that even so many years after Stalin, the real biography of this Yusuf II and the impact of Stalinism has yet to be written. In my *In the Name of Marx,* I had said that Stalinism in the erstwhile Soviet Union represented not mere ideological unclarity, but created a Master Representation where the world communist movement succumbed to the totalitarian Stalinist ideological prison house. This Stalinist prison house has become the *big Other* (to borrow a Lacanian term from Žižek) for the world communist revolution. It is not capitalism that has defeated revolution, but this awful *big Other*. And this Stalinist big Other would create the Phantasmagorical Revolution without a Revolution. But there is more to this Revolution without the Revolution, and that is the counterrevolution against the Leninist theory and praxis of the party, a counterrevolution perfected by Stalin, speaking however in the name of Lenin. It must be noted that a counterrevolution took place against Marx. Now we shall see a counterrevolution against Lenin that speaks in his name. The Indian comrades would, by and large, follow the path given by Stalin. Lenin's revolutionary theme of the dialectics of spontaneity and intellectual work in the masses in his *What is to be Done?* was and is yet today totally absent from the understanding of the Indian Left. But there is more to the Stalin question than those of philosophical importance.

On December 24, 1922, an ailing Lenin (he was shot in the head by Dora Kaplan) dictated notes that go as the 'Letter to the Congress' where he says:

> Our Party relies on two classes and therefore its instability would be possible and its downfall inevitable if there were no agreement between those two classes. In that event this or that measure, and generally all talk about the stability of our C.C., would be futile. No measure of any kind could prevent a split in such a case. But I hope that this is too remote a future and too improbable an event to talk about.
>
> I have in mind stability as a guarantee against a split in the immediate future, and I intend to deal here with a few ideas concerning personal qualities.
>
> I think that from this standpoint the prime factors in the question of stability are such members of the C.C. as Stalin and

> Trotsky. I think relations between them make up the greater part of the danger of a split, which could be avoided, and this purpose, in my opinion, would be served, among other things, by increasing the number of C.C. members to 50 or 100.
>
> Comrade Stalin, having become Secretary-General, has unlimited authority concentrated in his hands, and I am not sure whether he will always be capable of using that authority with sufficient caution. Comrade Trotsky, on the other hand, as his struggles against the C.C. on the question of the People's Commissariat for Communications has already proved, is distinguished not only by outstanding ability. He is personally perhaps the most capable man in the present C.C., but he has displayed excessive self-assurance and shown excessive preoccupation with the purely administrative side of the work.[10]

Lenin was talking of the dangers of split in the party. But the dangers of a split were not related only to the perception of Stalin as having an authoritarian personality, but related to the understanding of the relation of authoritarianism to the class structure of society. There is, however, another important question when one is reading this famous 'Letter to the Congress', namely, the question of dialectics. Consider Lenin:

> Speaking of the young C.C. members, I wish to say a few words about Bukharin and Pyatakov. They are, in my opinion, the most outstanding figures (among the younger ones), and the following must be borne in mind about them: Bukharin is not only a most valuable and major theorist of the Party; he is also rightly considered the favourite of the whole Party, but his theoretical views can be classified as fully Marxist only with the great reserve, for there is something scholastic about him (he has never made a study of dialectics, and, I think, never fully appreciated it).[11]

There are two conclusions that one derives from the above quotes, one that Stalin represented authoritarianism of the worst kind (all the comrades that Lenin mentions in the letter were killed by Stalin), and the other concern is the question of dialectics, especially that of Hegelian dialectics and its relation to Marxism that concerned Lenin at least since 1914. But why does one, so the reader may ask, talk of dialectics and Stalin after talking of dramaturgy, when one is talking of the question of Left politics, especially in India? We are mentioning this because it is Stalinism (or if it is not the brutal kind of Stalinism, then it is the marriage of liberalism with Stalinism) and the lack of the understanding of dialectics that remain the core of Established Left politics in India till date.

At a superficial level, one may say that Stalin and Stalinism emerged because the world revolution retreated and one had to (at any costs, albeit even in totalitarian and murderous ways) defend this revolution. Thus it could only be authoritarianism that could save the revolution. But this view point would not only be an apologia for mass murder of communists, but completely unscientific and wrong. *Stalinism means the utter fear of revolution.* To understand Stalinism one turns once again to Žižek:

> The entire history of the Soviet Union can be comprehended as homologous with Freud's famous image of Rome, a city whose history is deposited in its present in the guise of the different layers of the archaeological remainders, each new level covering up the preceding one, like (another model) the seven layers of Troy, so that history, in its regression towards ever older epochs, proceeds like the archaeologist, discovering new layers by probing deeper and deeper into the ground. Was the (official ideological) history of the Soviet Union not the same accumulation of exclusions, of turning persons into non-persons, of the retroactive rewriting of history?[12]

The active sabotaging of international revolutions along with the falsification of history is the essence of Stalinism. Therefore when Trotsky writes *The Stalin School of Falsification* he was not altogether incorrect. It is thus necessary to create a typography to understand Stalinism. And this is why I am saying that by Stalinism I mean the counterrevolution in the Soviet Union after Lenin's death where the New Economic Policy (NEP) bureaucrats replaced the grassroots communists followed by the massacre of the Old Bolsheviks. These NEP bureaucrats imagined that they became the "managers of the Russian Revolution". In actuality they were the "managers of the counterrevolution". It is obvious that these NEP men were not revolutionaries in any sense of the term, and most certainly not the professional revolutionaries that Lenin advocated in his *What is to be Done?* Thus it is important to understand that the fear of World Revolution and the active attempt to sabotage World Revolution is an essential feature of Stalinism. The massacre of the Shanghai communists by Chiang

Kai-shek in 1927 is an example of the fear of the World Revolution and the capitulation to the class enemy. Stalin knew that any revolution would displace the bureaucratic Thermidor. Stalin's role has been infamous in the alliance with the Kuomintang led by Chiang Kai-shek and the consequent suppression of the Chinese Soviets.

This is what Stalin in his typical rhetoric way said. Note for him, any autonomous action of the Chinese proletariat was foolish and the Chinese communists had to be appendages of the Kuomintang. Note this Stalinist rhetoric:

> Chiang Kai-shek is submitting to discipline. The Kuomintang is a bloc, a sort of revolutionary parliament, with the Right, the Left, and the Communists. Why make a coup d'etat? Why drive away the Right when we have the majority and when the Right listens to us? ... At present, we need the Right. It has capable people, who still direct the army and lead it against the imperialists. Chiang Kai-shek has perhaps no sympathy for the revolution but he is leading the army and cannot do otherwise than lead it against the imperialists. Beside this, the people of the Right have relations with the General Chang Tso-lin [the Manchurian warlord] and understand very well how to demoralize them and to induce them to pass over to the side of the revolution, bag and baggage, without striking a blow. Also, they have connections with the rich merchants and can raise money from them. So they have to be utilized to the end, squeezed out like a lemon, and then flung away.[13]

Merely laughing at the absurdity of using the rightists and then arrogantly claiming that the right-wing can be "utilized to the end, squeezed out like a lemon, and then flung away" would simply be not enough. For one, the above statements make no sense at all. If they make sense then it obvious what Stalin's politics was—class collaboration, of course. What does Stalin say? He says that the "Kuomintang is a bloc, a sort of revolutionary parliament, with the Right, the Left, and the Communists." One may ask: Is the Kuomintang a "revolutionary parliament"?

Also note from the above quote: "…we need the Right. It has capable people, who still direct the army and lead it against the imperialists." This means that the Chinese rightists would fight the imperialists. This is Stalin's theory of imperialism. Stalin's argument of needing the rightists was not an isolated statement.

His need for the right-wing was essential for his own survival. Disarming revolutionaries in front of class enemies would be suicide. But even more suicidal would be to imagine that the rightists are "capable people" who could fight imperialists. But with the disarming of the revolutionaries, suicide it was. A few days later on April 12, 1927 after Stalin's infamous speech, Chiang Kai-shek massacred thousands of the vanguard fighters of the Chinese Revolution. Stalin's thesis was that of the Menshevik Martynov who had outlined his theory of class collaboration. In fact just a few days before Chiang Kai-shek's coup, the *Pravda* proclaimed that China was not run by a bourgeois government, but by a "government of the bloc of four classes."[14] The line of class collaboration, in fact collaboration with right-wing class enemies was carried out with full force in the Stalinist era, as is evident by Kalinin's speech on March 6 1927, followed by Rudzutak's speech on March 8, culminating in Stalin's speech on April 5, 1927.[15] What was happening is that one was "trampling underfoot the fundamental principles of Marxism"[16]. "The Left should have had the power", so Trotsky said, "but finally lost it."[17] The essence of losing power is to be found in Stalinism. Stalinism breeds only on class collaboration. It takes the form of the "bloc of four classes". But it is at best merely a "pompous title".[18] This, however, could be much more dangerous than merely pomp. Trotsky writing a few days after the massacre said that he "found the photograph of Chiang Kai-shek sent through the Eastern department of the ECCI and the request promptly to send him my autographed picture."[19] But why did this happen? Why this "thoroughly comprising matter"?[20] Is this not a "malicious irony of fate" that the portrait was sent on the eve of the slaughter?[21]

Stalin's political stance was on the impossibility of creating the soviets in China. His reason was that the soviets were created to fight the tsar and since there was no tsar in China, there was no need for them.[22] But probably the most "ideological" part of Stalinism is the theological interpretation of Marxism where Marxism was declared a "science" which studies "laws" which "take place independently of the will of man". What does this mean? Does it mean that the slaughter was to be understood as authored by the "hidden hand" of fate? Consider Stalin's *Economic Problems of Socialism in the USSR* which outlined this theological version of socialism. According to this treatise:

> Man may discover these laws, get to know them, study them, reckon with them in his activities and utilize them in the interest of society, but he cannot change or abolish them. Still less can he form or create new laws of science.[23]

"Laws" here for Stalin had two interpretations. One the "law" of theology as set by the invisible hand of the gods and revealed to the prophets. The other is the idea of "law" in the positivist idea of the sciences.

But what law is Stalin talking of? He is talking of the law of value that regulates and governs commodity production and the functioning of classes. So when he says that one cannot abolish laws, he means that one cannot abolish the law of value, commodity production and classes. Consequently for Stalin, value, commodity production and classes will always remain. Consider Stalin:

> The same must be said of the laws of economic development, the laws of political economy—whether in the period of capitalism or in the period of socialism. Here, too, the laws of economic development, as in the case of natural science, are objective laws, reflecting processes of economic development which take place independently of the will of man. Man may discover these laws, get to know them and, relying upon them, utilize them in the interests of society, impart a different direction to the destructive action of some of the laws, restrict their sphere of action, and allow fuller scope to other laws that are forcing their way to the forefront; but he cannot destroy them or create new economic laws.[24]

What has to be noted is the utter disregard of revolutionary praxis that Stalin advocated. Note now how this thesis is the exact opposite of what Marx advocated when he said that:

> The chief defect of all hitherto existing materialism—that of Feuerbach included—is that the thing [*Gegenstand*], reality, sensuousness, is conceived only in the form of the *object [Objekt] or of contemplation [Anschauung]*, but not as *sensuous human activity, practice*, not subjectively.....Hence he (we should say "Stalin", M.J. my addition) does not grasp the significance of "revolutionary," of "practical-critical," activity.[25]

Further:

> The question whether objective [*gegenständliche*] truth can be attributed to human thinking is not a question of theory but is a practical question. Humanity must prove the truth—i.e. the reality and power, the this-sidedness [*Diesseitigkeit*] of his thinking in practice. The dispute over the reality or non-reality of thinking that is isolated from practice is a purely *scholastic* question.[26]

And since Stalin thought that "one cannot change or abolish them (laws)" and yet since change had to be brought, it was brought from the "outside":

> Hence, this doctrine necessarily arrives at dividing society into two parts, of which one is superior to society (Robert Owen).[27]

One could replace the name of Owen with Stalin. And of course, Stalin would never have learnt the following:

> The philosophers have only *interpreted* the world in various ways; the point, however is to *change* it. [28]

It is obvious that to change the world, would imply overthrowing the Stalinist Thermidor. But this Bonapartist Thermidor would create a colossal authoritarian state along with the creation of the myth of socialist commodity production and the ideology of Great National Chauvinism. Thus:

> While a large part of the Indian Left inherited the above stated Stalinist baggage, what marks them off is their fetish for bureaucratic empiricism that may not be *actively* counterrevolutionary, but because of its unconscious and unwitting *Stalinist goal of capitalism without the capitalists*, post-Stalin Stalinism (which includes the Parliamentary Left) would be essentially pro-capitalist, nationalist and consequently against internationalism and the praxis of the international proletariat. It is necessary to state that the Indian Left has also been married to Nehruvian liberalism. It is these two souls—of Stalin and Nehru—that are locked in the unfortunate breast of the Parliamentary Left. And like Faust they would inevitably be hurled into their capitalist hell. And in this capitalist hell they would not find the damned anti-Christ Trotsky but the saint Stalin himself.[29]

The Established left is correct when it chides the Indian fascists for distorting history. But what about their own distortions that "weigh like a nightmare", to recall Marx once again, "on the brain of the living"?[30] Cannot the Indian Left simply wake up from this nightmare that fantasizes that Trotsky signified the Jewish anti-Christ? Why this active repression in understanding revolutionary history? Let us recall Žižek here:

> One is tempted to risk the parallel with Freud's distinction between primordial (founding) and secondary repression in the unconscious: Trotsky's exclusion amounted to something like the 'primordial repression' of the Soviet state, to something that cannot ever be readmitted through 'rehabilitation', since the entire order relied on the negative gesture of exclusion. Trotsky is the one for whom there is no place either in pre-1990 really-existing socialism or post-1990 really-existing socialism in which even the communist nostalgiacs do not know what to do with Trotsky's permanent revolution—perhaps the signifier 'Trotsky' is the most important designation of what is worth redeeming in the Leninist legacy.[31]

If one talks of the essential difference between Lenin and Stalin, it is also necessary to talk of the difference between Trotsky and Stalin. Consider Žižek once again:

> In Stalin 'Lenin lives forever' as an obscene spirit which 'does not know it is dead', artificially kept alive as an instrument of power. In Trotsky, the dead Lenin continues to live like Joe Hill—he lives wherever there are people who still struggle for the same Idea.[32]

One must understand these differences in order to understand twentieth century Marxism and what happened to the Soviet Union after Lenin's death in 1924. It is then that we understand the terrible Stalinist counterrevolution, a counterrevolution that was dressed in revolutionary attire which happened to fool the world in the last century and which yet happens to fool the world. And if it does not fool the entire world, it at least fools a dominant part of political Marxism even today. And to understand the Stalinist counterrevolution one has to study the minutest details that happened in Soviet history. Joseph Hansen in the foreword to *Stalin's Frame Up System* said that "of the nine people who were members of the Political Bureau during Lenin's lifetime, i.e. actual rulers of the fate of the USSR there remains only one unaccused, Stalin."[33] All the rest were accused by Stalin and his henchmen of being fascist agents. So how did it happen that everyone in the top leadership of the Bolsheviks were—according to Stalinist imagination—enemies of the Revolution, in fact fascist agents? How did Trotsky, Bukharin, Zinoviev, Kamenev (the list is just too long) work for some secret fascist organization by starting a revolution in 1917, besides working for international communism all their lives? Was Stalin just a psychotic and paranoid thug or was there something beyond paranoia? Can one then talk of Hegel's *die List der Vernunft* or "the cunning of reason" where reason became a destruction of reason? Or is there also something more to this? Was Stalin then a fascist? Was Stalin's pointing a finger of suspicion to the Old Bolsheviks (claiming that they were fascists) actually a ruse to veil his own fascism?

For this one needs empirical evidence. When Stalin was framing all the comrades in the infamous Moscow Trials in the late 1930s it was the Italian fascist Mussolini who said:

> Stalin renders a commendable service to fascism.[34]

One has to note the details of actual history in order to understand how Stalin indeed did "commendable service to fascism". The trials took place in the late 1930s when fascism was getting ready for war. After all, what sort of an imbecile was Stalin that, when fascism which had sworn to tear down international communism, instead of closing ranks goes on a mass murder spree against what would have been his comrades? Note Sydney Hook, apparently no friend of Trotsky or the Trotskyite idea of international revolution:

> The charges against the defendants were mind-boggling. They had allegedly plotted and carried out the assassination of Kirov on December 1, 1934, and planned the assassination of Stalin and his leading associates—all under the direct instructions of Trotsky. This, despite their well-known Marxist convictions concerning the untenability of terrorism as an agency of social change. Further, they had conspired with Fascist powers, notably Hitler's Germany and Imperial Japan, to dismember the Soviet Union, in exchange for the material services rendered by the Gestapo. In order to allay the suspicion flowing from the Roman insight that no man suddenly becomes base, the defendants were charged with having been agents of the British military at the very time they or their comrades

> were storming the bastions of the Winter Palace. In addition, although the indictment seemed almost anticlimactic after the foregoing, they were accused of sabotaging the five-year plans in agriculture and industry by putting nails and glass in butter, inducing erysipelas in pigs, wrecking trains, etc...... Despite the enormity of these offences, all the defendants in the dock confessed to them with eagerness and at times went beyond the excoriations of the prosecutor in defaming themselves. This spectacular exercise in self-incrimination, unaccompanied by any expression of defiance or asseveration of basic principles, was unprecedented in the history of any previous Bolshevik political trial.[35]

Why and how these Bolsheviks confessed is perplexing. Why did they confess to bizarre crimes created by the Stalinist imagination? Was this "confession" a Biblical sort of atoning for one's sins (real or imaginary) before a priest? Did Stalin—remember Stalin was a trained priest—take this medieval type of confession from feudal Europe whereby he transformed the spectacle of the feudal burning of witches into the mass execution of the Bolsheviks? Was Stalin a fascist of a brutal medieval type?

In 1922 Lenin writing a letter to Kamenev 'On the Establishment of the USSR' viewed Stalin as "somewhat hasty".[36] In the same year he talks of "Stalin's haste", not to forget his "spite".[37] "In politics spite", so Lenin continues, "plays the basest of roles"[38]. Lenin talks of internationalism. But internationalism cannot simply bypass the "national question". Consequently:

> A distinction must necessarily be made between the nationalism of the oppressor nation and that of the oppressed nation, the nationalism of a big nation and that of a small nation.
>
> In respect of the second kind of nationalism we, nationals of a big nation, have nearly always been guilty, in historic practice, of an infinite number of cases of violence; furthermore, we commit violence and insult an infinite number of times without noticing it. It is sufficient to recall my Volga reminiscences of how non-Russians are treated; how the Poles are not called by any other name than Polyachiska, how the Tatar is nicknamed Prince, how the Ukrainians are always Khokhols and the Georgians and other Caucasian nationals always Kapkasians.
>
> That is why internationalism on the part of oppressors or "great" nations, as they are called (though they are great only

in their violence, only great as bullies), must consist not only in the observance of the formal equality of nations but even in an inequality of the oppressor nation, the great nation, that must make up for the inequality which obtains in actual practice. Anybody who does not understand this has not grasped the real proletarian attitude to the national question, he is still essentially petty bourgeois in his point of view and is, therefore, sure to descend to the bourgeois point of view.

What is important for the proletarian? For the proletarian it is not only important, it is absolutely essential that he should be assured that the non-Russians place the greatest possible trust in the proletarian class struggle. What is needed to ensure this? Not merely formal equality. In one way or another, by one's attitude or by concessions, it is necessary to compensate the non-Russian for the lack of trust, for the suspicion and the insults to which the government of the "dominant" nation subjected them in the past.

I think it is unnecessary to explain this to Bolsheviks, to Communists, in greater detail. And I think that in the present instance, as far as the Georgian nation is concerned, we have a typical case in which a genuinely proletarian attitude makes profound caution, thoughtfulness and a readiness to compromise a matter of necessity for us. The Georgian [Stalin] who is neglectful of this aspect of the question, or who carelessly flings about accusations of "nationalist-socialism" (whereas he himself is a real and true 'nationalist-socialist', and even a vulgar Great-Russian bully), violates, in substance, the interests of proletarian class solidarity, for nothing holds up the development and strengthening of proletarian class solidarity so much as national injustice; "offended" nationals are not sensitive to anything so much as to the feeling of equality and the violation of this equality, if only through negligence or jest—to the violation of that equality by their proletarian comrades. That is why in this case it is better to over-do rather than undergo the concessions and leniency towards the national minorities. That is why, in this case, the fundamental interest of proletarian class struggle, requires that we never adopt a formal attitude to the national question, but always take into account the specific attitude of the proletarian of the oppressed (or small) nation towards the oppressor (or great) nation.[39]

Just as the Austrian Adolf Hitler in the name of German supremacy massacred millions, so too the Georgian Iosif (Yusuf) Stalin in the name of Russian chauvinism inflicted irreparable damage to the world communist movement. The "'orientalization' of the revolution's mental and political climate", to borrow a phrase of Isaac Deutscher was taking place.[40] In 1922 itself the "truly Great-Russian nationalist campaign" was going on, for which Stalin and Dzerzhinsky would be to blame.[41]

The civil war made the Bolshevik Revolution turn towards a form of militarization, albeit a revolutionary militarism under Trotsky. "War is politics by other means" so Clausewitz's celebrated statement went. What would soon happen is that politics would become a form of war, dirty and merciless. Deutscher said that "when in the middle of March 1918, Trotsky was appointed Commissar of War and President of the Supreme War Council, he did not even put down his pen to take up the sword—he used both."[42] Further "he undertook to conjure an army out of an apparent void".[43] From the void the concrete Red Army came into being. Stalin did not have to conjure anything. He merely had to take over the concrete. For that the chopping of Trotsky's head was necessary.

Further, with Trotsky, the "'orientalization' of the revolution's mental and political climate" could not take place. He was too much of a world revolutionary for the spectre of the Oriental despot to overcome him. For the crown of the Oriental despot to fit the head of the now heralding counterrevolution, an Oriental head was necessary. The crown would fit on Stalin's head.

There are four main characters in this work:

Yusuf I: The messianic hero, the misunderstood revolutionary and lover.

Zuleika: The international revolutionaries, betrayed by the false Yusuf(s).

Yusuf II: Stalin.

Yusuf III: Gandhi.

2
Main Text

Combat or death, bloody struggle or extinction.
Thus the question is inexorably put.

Karl Marx quoting George Sand

Liberalism, rotten to the core, tries to revive itself in the form of socialist opportunism. The period of preparation of the forces for great battles, is interpreted by them as the renunciation of these battles. Improvements in the position of the slaves enabling them to carry on a fight against wage-slavery is explained by them in the sense that the slaves are selling their liberty rights for a penny.

V.I. Lenin

Saints should always be judged guilty until proven innocent.

George Orwell

Introduction

In the words of Herbert Marcuse the 1917 Bolshevik Revolution was a "radical act", while in the words of Alain Badiou it was an "Event" of messianic-redemptive character. In contrast to this radical rendering, the 1917 Revolution gave way to what the anti-revolutionary Russian novelist Mikhail Bulgakov called the "enigmatic unknown future".[44]

While Marcuse and Badiou, clearly philosophers of human emancipation, stand for the path of the communist revolution, Mikhail Bulgakov author of the celebrated novel *The Master and*

Margarita stood on the other side of the philosophical barricades. For him:

> The time of reckoning has begun. Inch by inch, the heroic volunteers [of the White Army] will tear the Russian land from Trotsky's hands....But there will have to be a lot of fighting and bloodshed, because as long as mad men whose heads have been turned by Trotsky stand with weapons in their hand, pawing the ground behind his sinister figure, there will be no life, but instead a fight to the death. We have to fight.[45]

The year 1917 clearly divided the world into "good" and "evil". It depended on one's class position and philosophical outlook on which side of the barricades one stood. On the one hand, we have "modern prophets" (to recall Bulgakov once again) who lead people to the "dreadful road", the road that could only end with the "malevolent disease [communism]"[46]. Communism, for Bulgakov, was not only a disease; it was a "malevolent disease". It will then be "spreading to the West and vanquishing it."[47] If there was a Russian disease, which by 1919 was spread by Trotsky, there was the West with its "countless lights" with "airmen (who) will thrust through the air they have conquered", "do research, publish and study"[48]. Both Russia and the West had to be saved from this disease called communism. And who would save them? It was Marcuse, who after the Nazi Holocaust, asked his onetime teacher Martin Heidegger why he identified with the Nazis and was "considered as one of the strongest proponents".[49] Marcuse goes on:

> Is this the way you would like to be remembered in the history of ideas? Every attempt to combat this cosmic misunderstanding founders on the generally shared resistance to taking seriously a Nazi ideologue. Common sense (also among intellectuals) which bears witness to such resistance, refuses to view you as a philosopher, because philosophy and Nazism are irreconcilable.[50]

To which Heidegger answered:

> Concerning 1933; I expected from National Socialism a spiritual renewal of life in its entirety, a recollection of social antagonisms and a deliverance of Western Dasein from the dangers of communism.[51]

Note the words: "deliverance of Western Dasein from the dangers of communism". Communism was and is yet a danger. Heidegger was at least honest in stating that philosophy is essentially political and philosophy as a bourgeois enterprise has to confront Revolutionary Marxism. For him Western civilization was in danger from the forces of Bolshevism. But it is not only a danger, as Bulgakov notes, it is a disease spread by the vermin Trotsky. Note that Bulgakov would see Trotsky as the revolutionary spreading the disease called "revolution". According to him, one should be aware of this dangerous disease. What has also to be noted is that besides the pro-czarist Bulgakov, Stalin would also conceive both Trotsky and Trotskyism as disease and vermin fit only to be destroyed. So what is common between Bulgakov, Heidegger and Stalin? They all know that revolution was not only a disease but primarily an evil spectre that needed to be exorcized.

To confront this revolutionary "Event", one had to invent a fairly tale of a disease spreading vermin-spectre. Recall Marx and Engels who had said that the popes and the czars, along with French ministers and radicals, joined by German police spies have concocted a "nursery tale" that good old Christian Europe is attacked by an anti-Christ vermin.[52] This is called the "spectre of communism" the spectre that is haunting Europe. Europe had to be saved from this spectre. Bulgakov noted this as did Heidegger.

But the conflict between Western Dasein (read "capitalism") and communism that we noted earlier which was defined as a struggle between good and evil would be resolved by an unknown force that was literally beyond good and evil. The force would be Stalinism. In this sense it is necessary to expose the great lie that Stalin saved the world from Nazism and fascism. In the aftermath of the notorious Moscow Trials when Stalin liquidated the Old Bolsheviks, it was John Dewey who recorded this lie[53] and Mussolini who supported it. But why did Mussolini support Stalin saying that he was doing great service to fascism? Was then Stalin a fascist if not an open one, then a secret fascist?[54]

If however, with the rise of Stalin by 1928, the wheel of history was turning backwards controlled as if by Hegel's "cunning of reason"; in India there was a different moving backwards, a different "cunning of reason" appeared with Gandhi appearing as an anti-colonial mass leader. Just as Iosif (Yusuf) Dzhugashvili was christened "Stalin" or the "man of steel", Gandhi would become the "Mahatma" or the "great soul". For the bourgeois national leaders—the native elites who sought to replace the colonial elites with the same caste and class structure of society—this "Great Soul" would be the unquestioned champion of the masses. But just as Trotsky disagreed with Stalin, in India, Gandhi would meet with a challenge. His name was B.R. Ambedkar who stood diametrically opposed to almost all the native elites. For him, Gandhi was no "Mahatma" no "great soul". He was just "Mr. Gandhi".

And if the czarist White Army and the Nazis would protect the elites from the dangers of communism, in India it would need someone else, someone who had to have a "great soul". Recently Perry Anderson penned his *The Indian Ideology* where he chides Gandhi as the counterrevolutionary par excellence. He rightly says that "all shades of political opinion in India, from the RSS to the CPM unite in formal reverence to a national icon".[55] The albatross rock that holds the Indian Left and which would soon sink them in the terrible ocean of capitalism and imperialism, fascism and counterrevolution would be the rocks of the two Yusufs, Yusuf II and Yusuf III, Stalin and Gandhi. We just saw that Yusuf II was a traitor to the Soviet revolution. We need to see the Indian Yusuf—the "Great Soul" or the Mahatma. Consider Ambedkar, the direct antithesis of not only Gandhi and the bourgeois leaders of the national movement, but the antithesis to the very reactionary ideology that Gandhi propagated:

> The Mahatma appears not to believe in thinking. He prefers to follow the saints. Like a conservative with his reverence for consecrated notions he is afraid that if he once again starts thinking, many ideals and institutions to which he clings will be doomed. One must sympathize with him. For every act of independent thinking puts some portion of an apparently stable world in peril. But it is equally true that dependence on saints cannot lead us to know the truth. The saints are after all only human beings, and as Lord Balfour said, "the human mind is no more a truth-finding apparatus than the snout of a pig." Insofar as he does think, to me he really appears to be prostituting his intelligence to find reasons for supporting this archaic social structure of the Hindus.[56]

In a sense Gandhi as Yusuf III, was not an ordinary counterrevolutionary. He would turn out to be an Indian version of Ayatollah Khomeini where (to borrow a phrase of Perry Anderson) "faith was subordinated to....politics".[57] Not only would faith supersede politics (subordinating it in the process) faith would be raised to the level of mass hysteria. While fascism had mastered this macabre "art" of creating mass hysteria, it was Gandhi who started this in India. Yet the Indian Left seems enamoured by this hysterical figure, just as it has been enamoured by the figure of Stalin. It is thus that one poses the question: Have the Indian Marxists ever understood Marx, ever understood what Revolution means? If they indeed did understand this, then they would not have fallen prey to Gandhi as the "guilt saint" that George Orwell talked of?[58] If the international revolution was destroyed by Yusuf II, we have another Yusuf, the Indian Yusuf, or Yusuf III, to be precise Mr. Gandhi who paraded himself as "Mahatma Gandhi". It is with these two counterrevolutionary figures of the two Yusufs that one begins the critique of the Established Left (unable to get out from their Stalinist cocoons), the Left who did not understand that both Yusufs would betray Zuleika. Zuleika is thus literally not only "love betrayed", but "revolution betrayed". Consider Orwell:

> In Gandhi's case the questions one feels inclined to ask are: to what extent was Gandhi moved by vanity — by the consciousness of himself as a humble, naked old man, sitting on a praying mat and shaking empires by sheer spiritual power — and to what extent did he compromise his own principles by entering politics, which of their nature are inseparable from coercion and fraud?... (It must be noted that, my insertion, M.J.) inside the saint, or near-saint, there was a very shrewd, able person who could, if he had chosen, have been a brilliant success as a lawyer, an administrator or perhaps even a businessman. ....The things that one associated with him—home-spun cloth, "soul forces" and vegetarianism—were unappealing, and his medievalist programme was obviously not viable in a backward, starving, over-populated country. It was also apparent that the British were making use of him, or thought they were making use of him.

The main issue here is to know how the freedom movement in India forgot all its promises of freedom to become an extended arm of global capital accumulation and how the Bolshevik Revolution turned into its direct opposite—unimaginable despotism. Yes 1947 was indeed "freedom at midnight", but freedom governed by capitalism. It is in this theoretical problematic that we note a two-fold crisis—the crisis following the 1917 Bolshevik Revolution and the crisis following the brutal partition of the Indian subcontinent from whence "freedom at midnight" emerged. And from this two-fold crisis emerged the two counterrevolutionaries (Yusuf II and III). While Raya Dunayevskaya and following her the Marxist-Humanists had identified Stalin as the figure of the anti-Bolshevik counterrevolution, and following the line of thinking from Trotsky to Perry Anderson who identified Gandhi as the Indian counterrevolutionary, a systematic study of these two counterrevolutionaries has not hitherto been done. The crisis of both the international communist movement and the Indian Left movement lies on the shoulders of these two counterrevolutionaries. It was, as if, in their craniums that the two counterrevolutions were formulated.

One needed a scientific imagination to grasp this. Since Stalin's takeover of power by the late 1920s, there was a crisis in both the Left movement in India and the world. Yet studies of these lacked rigorous dialectics. There was thus a certain form of "gap" seen where the very idea of revolution was seemingly absent from the analysis of the Left which was bred on not only Stalinist revisionist ideas, but bred on ideas that could not understand the dynamisms of world revolutions. On a closer look one found that this was no mere gap, this was a major error.

One actually needed discussions where debates and counter-debates would take place. But these never took place. These debates were thus absent debates, but not formless ones. It had to be formed. But then was it formed? And then something else got formed. 2014 and 2017 happened in India and the USA and the Left cried out that fascism has come both nationally and internationally.[59] The Left wanted a Lenin to fight fascism. But then (as we know) Lenin (i.e. the real Lenin) died before the advent of international fascism and before the triumph of fascism. The Left knew by now that Stalin and Mao are redundant. A new idea was needed for the Indian Left. But the cranium of the Established Left never allowed this to come to fruit since there is more of classical revisionism and thus more of Eduard Bernstein and Karl Kautsky than Lenin and Rosa Luxemburg in both their theory and praxis.

Instead of the imagined New Democratic Revolution of the Established Left, one witnessed the intensification of the speed and wrath of global finance capital and the explosion of global capitalist contradictions. The Islamic State in Syria and Iraq spread the wrath of mindless modernist theology in West Asia. If finance capitalism brought the Islamic State to power in parts of West Asia, the 2014 National Elections in India saw the replacement of the Congress led United Progressive Alliance with the BJP led alliance. Some saw this as a triumph of fascism. Some saw this as the victory of the Corporate Managerial State which would put up banners of anti-secular and anti-democratic politics, but also put up banners of pro-imperialism. Others said that the calls of wanting to create what the political elites call the "Hindu Rashtra" or the "Hindu Nation" was essentially modelled after the Nazi Third Reich. They said that this is an open threat to Constitutional Democracy in India and the single biggest challenge to the Indian Left. But none of these voices ever said what communism is and what the alternative to capitalism and fascism would be like. At best the Indian Left cried foul on those now in power and pictured a form of liberal secular democracy as its model.

We heard from the Indian Left that the new model of society and governance is based on the racist supremacist ideology of German Nazism, along with their caste supremacist tendency. But this comparison did not actually excite the political sensibilities of the Indian masses. The Left also said that with the rule of Zionist Israel, Zionism which has now become a dominant language of the Indian elites would be brought into its political baggage and would bring in the politics of one nation, one people, one language, along with the policy and practice of eliminating minorities. The Left also said that this form of authoritarian, racist and militarist tendencies have always been at the core of the theory and practice of fascism.

The questions that would emerge would be: Is fascism the prime concern for the Left, or should Marxism be chalking out a radical alternative to capitalism and imperialism and its entire baggage of liberalism and fascism? After all, do not the Congress and its liberal capitalist bandwagon also not say that fascism is bad, especially when they are not in power? But then is liberalism good? What then is liberalism? The liberals would say that all that they do is good and all which they do not like is fascism. After all, have not the global liberals repeatedly said ad infinitum, that fascism is authoritarianism just as communism is authoritarian? Have not the liberals for more than a century said that both fascism and communism are the enemies of an open society and the international community? Consider Trotsky:

> Agents of the British government depict the matter as though the war will be waged for principles of "democracy" which must be saved from fascism. All classes and peoples must rally around the "peaceful" "democratic" governments so as to repel the fascist aggressors. Then "democracy" will be saved and peace stabilized forever. This gospel rests on a deliberate lie. If the British government were really concerned with the flowering of democracy then a very simple opportunity to demonstrate this exists: let the government give complete freedom to India. The right of national independence is one of the elementary democratic rights. But actually, the London government is ready to hand over all the democracies in the world in return for one tenth of its colonies. If the Indian people do not wish to remain as slaves for all eternity, then they must expose and reject those false preachers who assert that the sole enemy of the people is fascism. Hitler and Mussolini are, beyond doubt, the bitterest enemies of the toilers and oppressed. They are gory executioners, deserving of the greatest hatred from the toilers and oppressed of the world. But they are, before everything, the enemies of the German and Italian peoples on whose backs they sit. The oppressed classes and peoples—as Marx, Engels, Lenin and Liebknecht have taught us—must always seek out their main enemy at home, cast in the role of their own immediate oppressors and exploiters. In India that enemy above all is the British bourgeoisie. The overthrow of British imperialism would deliver a terrible blow at all the oppressors, including the fascist dictators. In the long run the imperialists are distinguished from one another in form—not in essence. German imperialism, deprived of colonies, puts on the fearful mask of fascism with its sabre teeth protruding. British imperialism, gorged, because it possesses immense colonies, hides its sabre teeth behind a mask of democracy. But this democracy exists only for the metropolitan centre, for the 45,000,000 souls—or more correctly, for the ruling bourgeoisie—in the metropolitan centre. India is deprived not

> only of democracy but of the most elementary right of national independence. Imperialist democracy is thus the democracy of slave owners fed by the lifeblood of the colonies. But India seeks her own democracy, and not to serve as fertilizer for the slave owners. Those who desire to end fascism, reaction and all forms of oppression must overthrow imperialism. There is no other road. This task cannot, however, be accomplished by peaceful methods, by negotiations and pledges. Never before in history have slave owners voluntarily freed their slaves. Only a bold, resolute struggle of the Indian people for their economic and national emancipation can free India.[60]

What I have tried to argue is that this difference between liberalism and fascism is extremely unscientific and a silly idea. These emerge from the cranium of the lazy leftist; the part-time imagined revolutionary that Lenin had chided in his *What is to be Done?* In fact what the Left needs to say is that one should welcome fascism since it speaks the truth of capitalism, just as one needs to frown on liberalism since it hides the brutalities of capitalism. *Fascism thus is honest capitalism, just as liberalism is dishonest capitalism. Fascism also hastens the revolution. And for this reason we prepare for fascism, a preparation that will lead to the overthrow of capitalism and imperialism.*

Bringing this idea of fascism being liberalism with a gun into the Indian context one says that there is no essential difference between Gandhi and Nathuram Godse (the right-wing Hindutva fanatic who murdered Gandhi) and that the crying of certain self-appointed Congress leaders that Godse and the Indian fascists killed the liberal and tolerant Gandhi is simply meaningless if not absurd. After all, should the Left be so bothered about the bourgeois politicians killing one another?

But there is something else that the Left has not thought about, and that there is no difference between fascism and liberalism for the Revolutionary Communist. Both *are* the same, they only *appear* to be different. They are both different forms of state power of the bourgeoisie and as state power need to be overthrown. It must be noted that liberals are no lovers of tolerance and liberty. They are of course no lovers of the proletariat. Instead as Marx had said as soon as the liberals come to power they "would immediately turn their newly acquired power against the workers."[61] Once in power they would "force back at once the workers, their allies in the struggles, into their former oppressed position".[62] The role that the liberals play can only be a "treacherous role".[63] So instead of liberalism's phantasmagoria of liberty, equality and fraternity, we have to inscribe the new words: "illusions, delusions and treachery". It is in this perspective that we follow Lenin in calling liberals "civilized hyenas" who are "whetting their teeth" on Asia.[64] Consider Lenin once again:

> The dialectics of history were such that the theoretical victory of Marxism forces its enemies to disguise themselves as Marxists. Liberalism, rotten to the core, tries to revive itself in the form of socialist opportunism. The period of preparation of the forces for great battles, is interpreted by them as the renunciation of these battles. Improvements in the position of the slaves enabling them to carry on a fight against wage-slavery is explained by them in the sense that the slaves are selling their liberty rights for a penny. In a cowardly manner they preach "social peace" (i.e. peace with slave-ownership), renunciation of the class struggle, etc. They have many adherents among socialist parliamentarians, the various officials in the labour movement, and the "sympathizing" intellectuals.[65]

Lenin's plea to the proletariat is neither to be "corrupted by liberalism" nor to be enslaved by the "tyranny of the trusts".[66] *What one needs to say is that liberalism "rotten to the core" (to recall the above quote) is fascism with a veiled gun while fascism is liberalism with a brazen gun.* It is after all the gun which is important. Liberalism and fascism are mere coats of paint of these guns. In this same tune it is necessary to say that *there is no difference between Gandhi and Godse. Gandhi was Godse without a gun while Godse was Gandhi with an open gun.*

It is not merely sad but tragic that the Left have been mindlessly tailing the bourgeois parties. It is also sad that they go in the defence of Gandhi. They forget what Leon Trotsky had said of Gandhi as the "fake leader and false prophet".[67] What the Established Left now inexorably tied to the parliament and its worship does is that divorces itself increasingly from the masses and the class struggle. When they cry foul with reference to fascism, firstly they never explain what fascism is and secondly they get involved in all types of class alliances and compromises with the bourgeoisie. It is in this context that one recalls Trotsky once again:

> Titanic and terrible events are approaching with implacable force. Mankind lives in expectation of war, which will, of course, also draw into its maelstrom the colonial countries and which is of vital significance for their destiny. Agents of the British government depict the matter as though the war will be waged for principles of "democracy" which must be saved from fascism. All classes and peoples must rally around the "peaceful" "democratic" governments so as to repel the fascist aggressors. Then "democracy" will be saved and peace stabilized forever. This gospel rests on a deliberate lie.[68]

Any scientific understanding and any critical and democratic politics would say that it is not the political and ideological superstructure that is important, but the very material base from whence springs the entire edifice of politics and ideology. Thus one cannot merely mutter angry phrases against the ruling elite, screaming on national television of intolerance. Instead one has to see that the macabre mask of fascism has the face of late imperialism in permanent crisis. Nor can one have a reductionist understanding of fascism as the "the open, terrorist dictatorship of the most reactionary, most chauvinistic, and most imperialist elements of finance capital" the definition that emerged from Georgoi Dimitrov.[69]

To deal with global capitalism in crisis and the complete collapse of any sort of democratic order, one has necessarily to reimagine Marxism, Marxism that was declared dead in 1991 thus has to be awakened as the *spectre of communism*. What I would also like to say is that it is not rationalistic-democratic politics that the Left needs to indulge in, but in the dramaturgy of the haunting and taunting spectre of communism. Communism, true, is humanism, but it has to appear as a spectre. Just as capitalism appears in the form of the gun, communism has to appear as a spectre. The class struggle is between the gun and the spectre.

In this age of the complete destruction of reason which heralds the era of permanent wars and riots, Marxism has to be resurrected and can only be resurrected as a spectre. Francis Fukuyama's messianic "end of history" thesis would wither away only with the resurrection of Marxism. Thus instead of talking of how the brave new world of liberalism has collapsed, one needs to talk directly to the masses. This time communism has to appear in human form. One thus needs to talk of the problems that the

Indian Left has been facing, especially after the retreat in the 2009 National Elections, followed by the loss of the 2011 State Elections in the state of West Bengal and the consequent decimation in the 2014 National Elections. Both the liberal democratic Congress Party and the Parliamentary Left got a thorough beating:

> But this defeat was constituted in a specific logic where the leaders of the Parliamentary Left have been playing Sancho Panza to the Congress's Don Quixote since independence. A new script of this tragicomedy was written. To defeat the BJP which won in the 1999 National Elections, the Parliamentary Left and the Congress got together as the United Progressive Alliance (UPA). In the period 2004-9 the good Sancho thought that he could influence the even better Don. Conjured programmes were drafted and new methods for the transition to socialism germinated in the minds of the speculative Stalinists. But Don Quixote besides being a liberal democrat whose vision was set on the horizons of the American Empire needed the Left to be thrown off their magnificent liberal ship. Don Quixote signed the forbidden Nuclear Deal with the Yanks and the Left instead of being thrown out of the Yankee ship, themselves jumped into the choppy waters of the imperialist ocean.[70]

The Established Left jumped into the ocean of imperialism when Manmohan Singh, the then Prime Minister of India, who inspired by liberalism went to the USA to sign the Nuclear Deal. The Left backed off from the UPA II government thereby letting the neoliberals totally in charge of the Indian state which in 2014 would be then be taken over by the Hindu nationalist BJP. This Indian Left inspired by the idea of a decaffeinated revolution, namely an imagined revolution that would be said to emerge from the bourgeois parliament, instead of going to the masses and explaining the relation between the Indian state and imperialism, severed relations with the government, of which they were an important part. This triggered the Congress Party moving rightwards, the space which would eventually be taken by the BJP in the 2014 General Elections. It is here that one needs to recall Slavoj Žižek who states:

> Nowhere is the dictum 'every history is a history of the present' more true than in the case of the French Revolution: its historiographic reception always closely mirrored the twists and turns of political struggles. The identifying mark of all kinds of

> conservatives is its flat rejection: the French Revolution was a catastrophe from its very beginning, the product of the godless modern mind, it is to be interpreted as God's punishment for the humanity's wicked ways, so its traces should be undone as thoroughly as possible. The typical liberal attitude is a differentiated one: its formula is '1789 without 1793.' In short, what the sensitive liberals want is a decaffeinated revolution, a revolution which doesn't smell of a revolution. Francois Furet and others thus try to deprive the French Revolution of its status as the founding event of modern democracy, relegating it to a historical anomaly: there was a historical necessity to assert the modern principles of personal freedom, etc., but, as the English example demonstrates, the same could have been much more efficiently achieved in a more peaceful way. Radicals are, on the contrary, possessed by what Alain Badiou called the 'passion of the Real': if you say A—equality, human rights and freedoms—you should not shirk from its consequences and gather the courage to say B—the terror needed to really defend and assert the A. However, it is all too easy to say that today's Left should simply continue along this path. Something, some kind of historical cut, effectively took place in 1990: everyone, today's 'radical Left' included, is somehow ashamed of the Jacobin legacy of revolutionary terror with its state-centralized character, so that the commonly accepted motto is that the Left, if it is to regain political efficiency, should thoroughly reinvent itself, finally abandoning the so-called 'Jacobin paradigm.' In our post-modern era of 'emerging properties,' chaotic interaction of multiple subjectivities, of free interaction instead of centralized hierarchy, of a multitude of opinions instead of one Truth, the Jacobin dictatorship is fundamentally 'not for our taste' (free the term 'taste' should be given all its historical weight, as the name for a basic ideological disposition). Can one imagine something more foreign to our universe of the freedom of opinions, of market competition, of nomadic pluralist interaction, etc., than Robespierre's politics of Truth (with a capital T, of course), whose proclaimed goal is 'to return the destiny of liberty into the hands of the truth'? Such a Truth can only be enforced in a terrorist manner.[71]

But would Žižek be correct here? It is here that the voice of Robespierre is heard:

> If the mainspring of popular government in peacetime is virtue, amid revolution it is at the same time virtue and

> terror: virtue, without which terror is fatal; terror, without which virtue is impotent. Terror is nothing but prompt, severe, inflexible justice; it is therefore an emanation of virtue. It is less a special principle than a consequence of the general principle of democracy applied to our country's most pressing needs.[72]

The Indian Left seeped in the binary logic of Aristotle's formal logic could not see that terror, or to be precise revolutionary terror is not tyranny, is not violence of the state. Of course Revolutionary Marxism outrightly rejects the alleged "peaceful path to communism". Revolutionary terror is the awakening of virtue, virtue in the form of the spectre of communism that was first outlined in the *Manifesto of the Communist Party*. This has to be understood in the text of the Revolution *with* a Revolution. Thus what has to be noted is that there is a clear difference between Revolutionary Marxism and revisionism, between a Revolution *with* a Revolution and a Revolution *without* a Revolution. The decaffeinated revolution that Žižek mentions is revolution, true, but a Revolution without a Revolution. In India we have truly inherited this decaffeinated revolution—the revolution that is not only stillborn, but a revolution which is impotent. And that is why I also said that one main reason for the crumbling of the Soviet Union is that it was built on the edifice of a decaffeinated revolution, a revolution that was perfected by Stalin, a perfection carried on from Khrushchev to Gorbachev. In India, we have more Stalins, Khrushchevs and Gorbachevs, than Lenins and Trotskys. In the Soviet Union it were these Stalins, Khrushchevs and Gorbachevs who did not have the courage to defend the revolution. But then the courage to start the revolution has also been lacking. The Indian comrades were thus revolutionaries without courage. To understand this psychotic fear of revolution by the Indian Left one had to see the deep logic of fear, fear that is perpetually locked in their parliamentary cranium.

The Indian revolutionaries wanted to look ahead, but the fear of the revolution—fear of both virtue and terror—would not only haunt them, this fear would torment them. It is to this fear that we turn to. But this fear is not mere fear in the abstract, it is also fear grounded in concrete reality. The figure would be of the Oriental despot, the despot who would devour souls without measure.

The material ground of this despotism is what one calls the "Indic variation of the Asiatic mode of production". In the Indian subcontinent the new order even post-1947 could not get rid of the old order, could not get rid of the despot who would head the awful caste system where caste as *status groupism* not only stunted economic and cultural growth, but promoted extremist and violent politics. For a scientific understanding of the Indic variation of the Asiatic mode of production it is necessary to see the weaving of caste and rank worship with the downgrading of both labour and the sciences. It was P.C. Roy (1861-1944), the man of the Bengal Renaissance who pointed out that the caste system led by the Brahmanical Overlords led to a stagnation of scientific thinking.

At this juncture it must be noted that by the Asiatic mode of production, one does not imply a static, a-historical society. Instead what we get from Marx's articles penned for the *New York Tribune* like the 'The British Rule in India' and later in *Grundrisse* and the almost unread *Ethnological Notebooks* is an altogether different mode of production, a mode that cannot collapse into European history. This is precisely what Marx said in his celebrated 1877 letter to the Narodniki Mikhailovsky and the 1881 letter to Vera Zasulich.[73] There is a precise dynamism here in these non-Western societies and these dynamisms have to be studied in detail. It is here that I will say that there has been no feudalism in India and the very idea that there was anything called "Indian feudalism" is most certainly wrong.

What we see instead is the Indic form of Caste Overlordship with its political economy and ideology of stagnancy. In Indian history both overlap and intersect and yet are distinct. The unfortunate thing is that the Indian freedom movement starting in the late nineteenth century distinctly suppressed this Indo-Iranian basis of Indian history to create a demographical "Hindu" India. And it was the Congress Party which was responsible for this.

Liberal democracy, conservatism and fascism in India appearing as Caste Overlordship takes this unfortunate latter form. While all three (liberal democracy, conservatism and fascism) want to suppress this West Asian past, the last totally erases all traces of its Persian past. It takes the form of brutal Brahmanism, State Landlordism and violent racism and casteism. Let us look at this mechanism of Caste Overlordship, economic stagnation, the rise of idealism and the downgrading of the sciences where "the ideological hegemony of Brahmanism contributed to the stagnation of Indian society", "by arresting the growth of science and technology", presented "not only a reinforcement of the caste-system in the country, but a demise of science and hence of advances in technology".[74]

And just as Marx said in his 'The British Rule in India' that caste is the locus which Indian society stands on, we need to explore this entirely new mode of production that the Indian Left refused (and yet refuses) to touch, just as it refuses to study the idea of the Asiatic mode of production, obsessed, as if, by the idea of "Indian feudalism". For the Indian left, India was either capitalist or feudal. And if it was neither, then it was semi-feudal. For them due to their mechanical view of history, caste was destined to die with the coming of capitalism and modernity. How wrong they would be.

The Indian Elites as Caste Overlords

The idea that caste is rooted in pre-capitalist society while seeming to be historically correct would turn out to be phantasmagorical if it is not contextualized in concrete material and social relations. One has to talk of what Anand Teltumbde calls the "persistence of caste".[75] In this sense caste as an apartheid type system does not exist only in pre-capitalism, but also in capitalism. One cannot forget that capitalism, needs pre-capitalist sectors in order to reproduce itself.[76] What one says is that Indian capitalism did not and can never annihilate caste, instead capitalism would fashion caste according to its own hideous image. But it not only reproduces capitalism, it also reproduces liberalism, conservatism, not to forget, the forms of proto-fascistic and fascistic consciousness. The real problem is that it has also been able to fashion the Left parties, intoxicated by Stalinism.

That is why it must be stated that the communist revolution and the anti-caste revolutions would have to be *simultaneous* revolutions. And here once again the Left in India is preoccupied with the mechanical outlook that then gives way to the "stages theory of history" where a mythical bourgeois revolution is said to precede the communist one. For them just as one had to be an ape in order to become fully human, so too one had to be bourgeois in order that one could become a communist.

Thus what I am saying is that the stages theory which declares a New Democratic Revolution to precede a Communist Revolution is totally alien to India. Instead I am identifying the caste-clan mode of production from whose womb evolves modern capitalism. While the caste-clan system is generally located as a necessary part of pre-capitalist India, it is also to be understood as a necessary part of capitalist India. The fact that caste also serves as the social, political and ideological forms for liberal politics in India has to be mentioned. What needs to be stated is modern India could never annihilate the caste system, but re-order it for the purpose of capital accumulation. The idea that capitalism would by its alleged law of history annihilate caste is totally false. Marx's statement that "the country that is more developed industrially only shows, to the less developed, the image of its own future",[77] cannot be interpreted as pre-capitalist social formations disappearing, just as they are said to have disappeared in advanced capitalist countries. It is with this noting that I turn to the question of the Indian elites as Caste and State Overlords where the idea of the state as sovereign, or the state "absolute landlord"[78] is now realized as the feudo-capitalist. What India like great parts of South Asia has witnessed is this form of feudo-capitalism governed by the Caste Overlord.

It is from this historical base whereby the Indian liberal democratic Patron State (the Gandhian-Nehruvian State) emerged. It claimed to be "democratic". In actuality it has the Caste Overlords controlling this "democracy". Democracy since independence is under siege. But how is it yet "under siege"? It is under siege because the Caste Overlords have developed and mastered this parasitical bureaucratic system. The Indian state thus is not a democratic state but the state governed by the "semi-barbarian, semi-civilized communities",[79] these caste-communities which manifest themselves as clan systems which create the structures of extreme hierarchy and the ideology of rank worship.

What I have said a number of times which I have highlighted as central to my *Why We Are Not Hindus* is that the totem of purity and the taboo of pollution rule the ideological guidelines of caste, while economic and cultural stagnation are its two main pillars. One follows Ambedkar in outlining the two principles of graded inequality and division of labourers as central to the mechanism of caste. In the principle of graded inequality various labouring-subaltern castes are unable to recognize their exploiter, but are themselves graded within themselves unequally. And in the principle of division of labourers, there is a marked internal division based on the ideology of caste-hierarchy. While the Left has almost not touched this understanding of caste, it is the liberals that saw caste as a progressive structure—Gandhi and Nehru were the chief proponents of this worldview. Not only did they recognize this fact, they perfected this. And this is precisely why Ambedkar saw the Congress as the most reactionary party which perfected these principles of graded inequality and division of labourers.

But caste as an apartheid system is also to be understood as racism, albeit of the South Asian variety, where the upper castes are not merely understood as being of higher biological stock and the lower ones considered as inferior, but actually cultivated as inferior. There is an actual everyday cultivation of making caste identities. When I am talking of casteism as a form of South Asian racism, I am also calling this "*schizophrenic racism*" where ranking in terms of "high" and "low", "pure" and "impure" forms its ontological basis. The tragic element is that even the lower castes imitate this model and imagine that they belong to a superior stock.

Fascism has perfected this politics of race superiority. What fascism has always wanted was to transform India into an ethno-religious racist state. Savarkar, Godse and Golwalkar based their right-wing politics of Hindutva—or making India into a Hindu nation—on the idea of race and racial superiority. But this does not mean that Gandhi and Nehru were free from this blame. True they were not fascists. They did not want to exterminate Muslims. But for them too this bourgeois European idea of "race" was sketched deep in their ideological cranium.

For Nehru caste was a type of "joint family".[80] Unlike Ambedkar who in his *Castes in India* saw caste as an "enclosed class",[81] Nehru understood caste as "an all-inclusive order without any common dogma and allowing the fullest latitude to each group".[82] The romanticism of caste by the Indian liberals made them completely blind to an oppressive system. For Nehru, caste was not seen as an apartheid system but as "trade unions or craft-guilds" governed by a "strong sense of solidarity".[83] The figures to lead India to freedom from British rule would be figures that refused to see caste as an oppressive organization. While Nehru was proud of his "distinctive Aryan features",[84] Gandhi was a:

> ...cross between a Jain-infected Hindu orthodoxy and late Victorian psychomancy, the world of Madame Blavatsky, Theosophy, *planchette* and the Esoteric Christian Union. The two were not connected as garbled ideas from the former—karma, reincarnation, ascetic self-perfection, fusion of the soul with the divine—found occult form in the latter. Little acquainted with the Hindu canon itself in his early years, Gandhi reshaped it through the medium of Western spiritualisms of the period. His one aim in life, he decided, was to attain *moksha*: that state of perfection in which the cycle of rebirth comes to an end and the soul accedes to ultimate union with God. 'I am striving for the Kingdom of Heaven, which is *moksha*,' he wrote, 'in this very existence.' The path towards it was 'crucifixion of the flesh', without which it was impossible to 'see God face to face' and become one with him. But if such perfection could be attained, the divine would walk on earth, for 'there is no point in trying to know the difference between a perfect man and God.' Then there would be no limit to his command of his countrymen: 'When I am a perfect being, I have simply to say the word and the nation will listen.' Crucifixion of the flesh, in this conception, meant far more than the vegetarian prohibitions prescribed by his caste background. Not in food, but sex lay the overriding danger to liberation of the soul. The violence of Gandhi's revulsion against carnal intercourse of any kind mingled Christian fears of sin with Hindu phobias of pollution. Celibacy was not just a duty for the dedicated few. It was enjoined on all who would truly serve their country. 'A man who is unchaste loses stamina, becomes emasculated and cowardly. He whose mind is given over to animal passions is not capable of any great effort.' If a married couple gratified these, it was still 'an animal indulgence' that, 'except for perpetuating the race, is strictly prohibited'. At the height of political mobilization, in 1920, even conjugal union was impermissible: all Indians must forgo sexual relations, as 'a temporary necessity in the present stage of national evolution'. Complete continence—*brahmacharya*—was of such transcendent importance that an involuntary ejaculation at the age of 65 was matter for an anguished public communiqué. At 77, testing himself by sleeping nude with his great-niece, he

> wrote: 'Even if only one *brahmachari* of my conception comes into being, the world will be redeemed.' If his conception was to be universally adopted, the logical result would be 'not extinction of the human species, but the transference of it to a higher plane'.[85]

If Gandhi had his theosophical fetishes, Nehru too was schooled in the theosophical way. Annie Besant herself performed the ceremony of initiation for the young teenaged Nehru.[86] This was not a passing phase. Consider this:

> I dreamt of astral bodies and imagined myself flying vast distances. This dream of flying high up in the air (without any appliance) has indeed been a frequent one throughout my life; and sometimes it has been vivid and realistic and the countryside seemed to lie underneath me in a vast panorama.[87]

Nehru continues, "I do not know how the modern interpreters of dreams, Freud and others, would interpret this dream."[88] One way to interpret Nehru's dream is to see how he was literally fleeing from real life. The *reality* is caste and the Asiatic mode of production. The dream is the fleeing from this reality and along with the theosophists flying in the skies. His disavowal of caste led him to two types of fantasies: one that caste is actually a trade union and second is the flying in the phantasmagorical air.

While studies on caste in India have a long history, the question as to why this terrible system led by the terrible despot is so internalized is never seriously questioned. For Marx, the question of the cultural and psychological part (and thus the ideological superstructure) was central for his analysis. His idea of the economic base determining the superstructure was not to be seen in a mechanical one way street.

We know that Engels in his 1890 letters to Josef Bloc and Conrad Schmidt, his 1893 letter to Frantz Mehring and his 1894 letter to W. Borgius talked of the dialectic of the base and the superstructure and he chided the economists (the economic reductionists) for their lack of dialectics. According to Engels:

> ...these gentlemen all lack dialectics. They always see only here cause, there effect. That this is a hollow abstraction, that such metaphysical opposition exist in the real world only during crisis, while the whole vast process goes on in the form of interaction—though of very unequal forces, the economic

> being by far the strongest, most primordial, most decisive—that hence everything is relative and nothing absolute—this they never begin to see. As far as they are concerned, Hegel never existed.[89]

And:

> The reflection of economic relations as legal principles is necessarily a topsy-turvy one: it goes on without the person who is acting conscious of it...(They do not see that) everything is upside down.[90]

So what is this upside down world, this world that is topsy-turvy, this inverted world? One must insist that one cannot read the above stated texts without understanding the logic of inversion and the critique of reification that Marx laid bare in his *Critique of Hegel's Doctrine of the State.* In this site we understand that this topsy-turvy world that Marx talks of is reification, a form of transfiguration where the real subject is made the predicate and vice versa. What this implies is that humanity is made a predicate for certain anti-humanist forces, like caste, class, private property and the state.

What one needs to do in the study of Caste Overlordship and the hegemony of the Caste Overlords is to relate this form of reification and dehumanization to the reification of consciousness that Lukács kept central to his *History and Class Consciousness.* Thus the question: "How is consciousness reified?" is related to the onset of neurosis and psychosis with the coming of capitalism. What late capitalism has done is that it has synthesized neurosis and psychosis as "neurosis-psychosis" and structured it as the fascist unconscious. In India, the liberals would never be able to take on fascism. And this is because of their obsession with Gandhi.

Is Gandhi India's Oriental Despot?

Why Gandhi has been celebrated by the elites from the Congress to the BJP and the Established Left has not been squarely understood. In this celebration of Gandhi, Ambedkar's radical critique of Gandhi is completely forgotten. Now it is well known that Gandhi, famously known as the "Mahatma", even the "father of the nation" not only justified the caste system saying that "the caste system has saved Hinduism from disintegration".[91] He also once said that "all killing is not *himsa*"[92] and he "alone can practise *ahimsa* who knows how to kill".[93] The Mahatma added: "You cannot teach *ahimsa* to a man who cannot kill. You cannot make a dumb man appreciate the beauty and the merit of silence"[94] and the "practice of *ahimsa* may even necessitate killing and that we as a nation have lost the true power of killing. It is clear", so the Mahatma continued "that he who has lost the power to kill cannot practise non-killing. *Ahimsa* is a renunciation of the highest type."[95]

Not only did Gandhi preach the strange, in fact very violent form of the metaphysics of ahimsa, he was clearly on the side of the propertied class. Consider him telling the landlords: "I shall be no party to dispossessing propertied classes of their private property without just cause... But supposing that there is an attempt unjustly to deprive you of your property, you will find me fighting on your side."[96] So what do we see? We see that Gandhi was an unquestionable supporter of the zamindars and the entire unjust system of private property. As a supporter of the landlords and capitalists the "Mahatma" could take on any role possible, from being the interlocutor with the British colonial authorities to being the agent of the landlords and capitalists who would bargain with the proletariat:

> I am working for the cooperation and coordination of capital and labour and of landlords and tenants....You may be sure that I shall throw the whole weight of my influence in preventing class war...No member will talk of expropriation or extinction of private property......That is the fundamental conception of Hinduism, which has years of penance and austerity at the back of the discovery of their truth. That is why while we had the saints who have burnt out their bodies and laid down their lives in order to explore the secrets of the soul, we have none as in the West who have laid down their lives in exploring the remotest or highest regions of earth.[97]

So how does Gandhi, the alleged man with the "great soul", be revealed as Yusuf III? Was Gandhi just an incompetent irrationalist in the service of Nehru who used him to mobilize the masses, or was he an irrationalist in the service of imperialism? Was he then also a supporter of the Indian variation of apartheid, knowing that the caste system was the social life-force of both the political economy of India as well its cultural, religious and ideological superstructure? Then is he not, as Yusuf III, the horrible Caste Overlord and the Oriental Despot whose crimes would parallel that of the Georgian counterrevolutionary? Was the partition of the Indian subcontinent not a terrible crime and was Gandhi not a part of this terrible melodrama? Would not Goethe's cry be also relevant for Gandhi? Should then we say:

> Should this torture then torment us
> Since it brings us greater pleasure?
> Were not through the rule of Gandhi
> Souls devoured without measure?

Then was Gandhi not like Timur and Stalin getting pleasure in tormenting torture? If Gandhi's alleged tormenting torture of partition was notorious, so was his tormenting torturous views on caste. Note Gandhi's strictures against Dalits getting knowledge, claiming that a Dalit is a "person without moral education, without sense, and without knowledge."[98] Gandhi here mimes Manu for whom a Śūdra is one who has "committed evil acts".[99]

But the most perverted form of the destruction of reason is found here:

> I believe that interdining or intermarriage are not necessary for promoting national unity. That dining together creates friendship is contrary to experience. If this was true there would have been no war in Europe... Taking food is as dirty an act as answering the call of nature. The only difference is that after answering the call of nature we get peace while after eating food we get discomfort. Just as we perform the act of answering the call of nature in seclusion so also the act of taking food must also be done in seclusion.[100]

Gandhi was not only an apologist for the caste system and the consequent perversion emanating thereon; he was also for the capitalist mode of production. On March 12, 1918 he wrote:

> Let us consider what the workers are likely to gain by breaking their oath. These days, any honest person in India can earn twenty to twenty-five rupees a month by intelligent work. The worst that can happen to a worker is that his employees may dismiss him and he may have to look for other work. A thoughtful worker should realize that he will get work anywhere after a few days' search.[101]

Further:

> One of my correspondents suggests that we should abolish the caste [system] but adopt the class system of Europe—meaning thereby I suppose that the idea of heredity in caste should be rejected. I am inclined to think that the law of heredity is an eternal law and any attempt to alter the law must lead us, as it has before led, to utter confusion. I can see very great use in considering Brahman to be always a Brahman through his life. If he does not behave himself as a Brahman, he will naturally cease to command the respect that is due to the real Brahman.[102]

What needs to be done here is to recognize that caste is a combination of a reality that is determined by a notorious ideology and political economy, thus it has a material, social and ideological base. And it is here that one brings in caste consciousness as what Marx once called (in a different context) "estranged mind",[103] where this "Indian mind" is realized as "neurosis-psychosis", a mental disease that was perfected by Gandhi. And it is this neurosis-psychosis that unleashed the "wild aimless, unbounded forces of destruction".[104]

I shall come to this rather strange combination of class, racism (as *schizophrenic racism*) and neurosis-psychosis that has given rise to both Gandhi's liberalism and Indian fascism. What I am saying is that caste combines both the sites of the economic base and the political and ideological superstructure of the reified-estranged mind. That is why I have brought in Marx's problematic of alienation, reification and fetishism that deals with this Indian form of capitalism in India where caste and its accompanying schizophrenia is not only preserved, but actively reproduced, albeit in modern, capitalistic forms. In this sense one agrees totally with Ambedkar who said:

> No matter what Hindus say, Hinduism is a menace to liberty, equality and fraternity.[105]

The Democratization of the Oriental Despots

What modern democracy did in India was that it did not annihilate caste. Instead, governed by the Caste Overlords, it made every Indian neurotic-psychotic. Let us look at a recent popular daily the *Hindustan Times* which reported a bizarre incident that happened in Punjab in the northern part of India in order to understand this strange disorder called "neurosis-psychosis":

> Nearly a week after an upper caste Jat Sikh farmer committed suicide on discovering that his bride's mother was a Dalit, his younger brother threatened to take the extreme step too if the widow is married to him or any cousin living in their native Khai village of this district. So deep runs the upper-caste supremacy in the Malwa belt of rural Punjab that 22-year-old Manpreet Singh Brar's younger brother, Kuldeep, 19, threatened to commit suicide if the family tried to solemnize the marriage of his brother's widow with any of his cousins too.[106]

This seems more from the pages of Freud's diaries on the rat man and the cases of Dora and little Hans. I am bringing in here the psychoanalytic concepts of neurosis and psychosis and then I am claiming that in late capitalism, neurosis (as the eternal recurrence of the self-same trauma) and psychosis (as the complete withdrawal from reality) reaches a new stage of "neurosis-psychosis". In early capitalism neurosis and psychosis were separate phenomena. In late capitalism dictated by finance capitalism, we see a new stage of mental illness called "neurosis-psychosis". Caste in this age of late capitalism perfects this strange phenomena called "neurosis-psychosis". Like the neurotic return of the self-same trauma, caste is negated only to return once again. Marx's celebrated statement that the Indian "self-sufficient communities that constantly reproduce themselves in the same form, and when accidentally destroyed, spring up again on the spot and with the same name"[107] is understood in this neurotic understanding of caste. There is certainly something wrong in the state of India and most certainly something wrong in the state of so-called "golden Indian civilization" if suicide replaces love, human reason and humanity. It is from this report that I shall put forth a scientific understanding of the caste question. In fact this above stated report on the neurotic-psychotic suicide event is not merely a journalist reporting on one isolated event. Instead one places it as what Alain Badiou calls the "Event", not a messianic "Event", but an "Event" of tragic proportions. Caste is thus an "Event" where everyday "events" take place. And when the "Event" is not completely erased, tragic "events" are bound to repeat themselves. We not only live through these tragic happenings. We experience them. They are bizarre, tragic and extremely avoidable. And yet we refuse to avoid them. We in fact pretend that caste does not exist. And when we do accept this tragic social structure that weighs like a nightmare on our brains and hearts, we refuse to accept this tragic character of Indian society. We remain both blind and deaf to this tragedy. We refuse to see it. We refuse to hear the cries of the oppressed. What happened in such circumstances is that the emergence of a radical humanism is rendered impossible and in the historical context the emergence of a radical bourgeois was suppressed that would challenge both colonialism and the Asiatic caste-clan system. What happened in such circumstances is that there was a stunting of the development of industrial capitalism. And along with this we found the stunting of the growth of the socialized proletariat. What one locates is the emergence of a very different kind of bourgeoisie in India from that of the emergence of the West European bourgeoisie, which did not have the "spirit of Protestant ethics", as the guiding doctrine of the bourgeoisie, emerged as a new ideology to meet the needs of a new world of rising capitalism. Here privilege and status were replaced by the celebrated theory of social contract which served as the judicial foundation of society. Science not only replaced religion as the dominant factor in giving shape to social ideas, but also delegitimized religion.

India, on the other hand, legitimatized religion. True, democracy came to India, but it was the democracy of the Caste Despots. This is because every Indian wants to be this despot.

On "Silent Blindness"

"Silent blindness" is a new disease that has afflicted many parts of India. It is rather a strange type of disease. Silence is related to the lack of speaking and hearing, while blindness is related to the lack of, or rather, the end of sight. In this new disease that has afflicted large parts of this country, silent blindness has afflicted not only the acts of speaking, hearing and seeing. It has affected the very act of thinking itself. One needs to study this disease that is playing havoc with our tongues, ears, eyes and minds.

In the *Economic and Philosophic Manuscripts of 1844*, Marx talks of phenomenology as a science (*die Wissenschaft*) which comprehends (*begreift*) the estranged human essence.[108] I am talking of the phenomenology of "silent blindness" and claiming that this strange disease is the disease that emerges from what Marx calls the estrangement of the human essence.

A small note on terminology is necessary so as not to confuse Marx as a theoretician of "human nature", i.e. a-historical "nature" in the abstract, estranged from concrete society and history. We know this and we know that this is bourgeois fiction. That is why I am saying that by human essence (*das menschliche Wesen*), one does not mean human nature. Human nature is not the human essence. The idea of the human essence is much broader than the idea of human nature. *Wesen* (essence) and *Natur* (nature) should not collapse into one another. In my *The Seductions of Karl Marx*, I had made a rigorous line of demarcation between these two discourses.[109] I had also said that scholars like Maximilien Rubel, Tom Bottomore, Norman Geras and also translations of Georg Lukács and Louis Althusser were wrong in equating the idea of the human essence with human nature. The idea of the human essence is a humanist idea, while that of human nature is basically a bourgeois idea dominated by metaphysical elements.

Problems emerge in emancipatory politics—Marxism and Ambedkarism are two examples—when the human core of their philosophies are not kept centre stage. In contrast to the "theoretical anti-humanism" (this is Althusser's term in *For Marx*[110]) of a certain kind of Marxism and in contrast to the liberal misinterpretations of Ambedkar, I am keeping humanism as Revolutionary Humanism centre to philosophical reasoning. It is this philosophical reasoning that argues for humanity freed from anti-humanistic structures—whether those of caste, class, patriarchy, capitalism, national chauvinism, xenophobia, racism, militarism, imperialism, etc.—that shall literally "cure" this strange disease of "silent blindness". As a certain kind of humanist psychotherapy, philosophical reasoning will also speak to this counterrevolution. The central counterrevolution that I am implying is that of the caste structure of society and its entire ideological and ritualistic superstructure fashionably called "Hinduism". This counterrevolution is headed by the Caste Overlord, sometimes dressed as a liberal, sometimes as a fascist. This counterrevolution led by the Caste Overlord appears as a ghost.

It recalls Shakespeare's *Hamlet.* It recalls thus Marcellus on seeing the ghost of the dead king wandering the dark nights of Denmark:

> Thou art a scholar; speak to, it Horatio......
> Question it, Horatio....[111]

It is thought that if one speaks to ghosts they may speak back. Thus after recalling Marcellus our discourse on the silent counterrevolution recalls Horatio pleading to the wandering ghost:

> Stay! speak speak! I charge, speak!

The ghost, in Shakespeare's tragedy, however disappears. Horatio speaks to the ghost, but the ghost does not speak back. It exits only to appear once again. It speaks when Hamlet appears.

> I am thy father's spirit;
> Doom'd for a certain term to walk the night, And for the day confin'd to fast in fires,
> Till the foul, crimes done in my days of nature
> Are burnt and purged away. But that I am forbid
> To tell the secrets of my prison-house....[112]

Our ghost of caste though appearing like the Shakespearean spectre is brutal, almost eternal-like. We must know the secrets of this prison-house. In this sense one may recall Ambedkar:

> I may seem hard on Manu but I am sure my force is not strong enough to kill his ghost. He, lives like a disembodied spirit and is appealed to, and I am afraid will yet live long.[113]

And when the ghost refuses to rest and insists on wandering around haunting humanity and when the ghost wears the robes and the crown of a dead king, the questions remain: How should we speak to the ghost? Will the ghost of the counterrevolution listen to us? Will we be able to exorcise this ghost? Or are we to pretend that the ghost is only an illusion and perhaps with the help of the liberal exorcist would one fine day, or night, simply vanish?

In order to understand this anti-democratic mythical culture of Brahmanism, let us look at the deep structures of this foundational myth that the Indian elites boast of. Note that it is one class of people who wield the Ideological State Apparatus. The upper caste elites—the Brahmans—have total monopoly of speaking. The proletarianized Śūdras can only be the feet. What is important to note, that even in modern India, this foundational myth is reflected. The Brahmans who comprise probably 3.5 percentage of the population of India, control the ideological and political apparatus like the bureaucracy, media, educational institutes, etc., along with the merchant class (the Vaiśyas) who fund amply this form of Indian capitalism. One should however point out that the dominant mode of production in India is capitalist of the underdeveloped type that Paul Baran, Andre Gunder Frank and Arghiri Emmanuel reminded us of. It is futile to talk of semi-feudalism and link it to the caste question.

While it is well known that liberal secularism has been oblivious to the questions of fascism and caste, and along with it oblivious to the question to the ideas of graded inequality and division of labourers; there is also an alternative understanding of democracy and revolution, ideas that were introduced by B.R. Ambedkar, the great revolutionary, radical democrat and master par excellence of the critique of both caste and capitalism whom both the Indian liberals and the Indian Marxists inspired by Stalinism (and their reductionist and Eurocentric fetishism of "class" devoid of concrete analysis) never bothered to understand. This, in a way, would be the biggest challenge for the Indian Left. And since the Indian Left ignored the caste question, their theory of fascism was nothing but the blind mimicking of the Comintern's definition of fascism as the "most terroristic dictatorship of finance capital". Finance capitalism would not be without its brain, soul and flesh. In India all three—the brain, soul and flesh—would be of caste and the fetish of rank worship. What European fascism did was that it attacked not only communism, but also attacked the entire tradition of the European Renaissance and the Enlightenment.

One could say that European Revolutions (especially the French Revolution) could take place only after the Renaissance and the Enlightenment. Likewise one is demanding an Indian Renaissance and Enlightenment. This Renaissance and Enlightenment would have to construct the idea of Marxist humanism, where the demand for a full human life is made the demand of communism. In contrast to this humanism, note the essential anti-humanism in the split personality and culture that Caste Overlordship creates. What is tragic in this narrative that in India, it is not caste that people want to annihilate. Instead everyone in India wants to become a Caste Overlord. The tragedy is that political democracy in India has not been able to eradicate this anti-democratic mythical culture even in the popular masses despite the great revolutionary movements unleashed since the last few centuries. Instead this anti-democratic character appearing as myth, also appears, to borrow the terminology of Walter Benjamin, as *Trauerspiel* or simply "mourning play". In India this form of mourning appears as a false sense of happiness and as I have said in *Why We Are Not Hindus* also appears in the terminology of Fredric Jameson as the "hysterical sublime". I call this anti-democratic mythical culture that transfigures the sense of mourning into the feeling of false happiness and hysterical sublimity as "fundamental ontology" (following Martin Heidegger's *Being and Time*), where myth replaces scientific reasoning and authoritarianism replaces democracy. The tragedy is that this essential ontological division that the fundamental ontology of Indian civilization offers is incorporated into the daily life-world. The fascists have been triumphant in the 2014 polls because of this anti-democratic ontological culture. And it is through the use of ritual (as Walter Benjamin reminds us in *The Work of Art in the Age of Mechanical Reproduction*) that this anti-democratic culture is able to reproduce itself, not only as a dominant ideology of the ruling classes, but also as an ideology that the masses have consented to.

A certain methodological remark is necessary here that locates the political economy of underdevelopment and the culture emanating thereon. India has never had feudalism. Most certainly it did not have a European kind of feudalism. One cannot thrust feudalism as a "universal" category that is applicable to all societies in the world. Instead it is with this Asiatic concept of caste-clan with its ideology of rank worship and bureaucratic overdetermination of the economy that attention must now turn. While Marxist thinkers like Sharad Patil in Maharashtra made a serious study of caste in India, followed by Gail Omvedt, the idea of the Asiatic mode of production that has produced rank worship and the parasitical bureaucracy (which are yet present) was apparently missing from their studies. Patil talked of feudalism, albeit in the modified forms of "feudalism from above" and "feudalism from below". The same error was made earlier by the great historian D.D. Kosambi. Here one needs to point out how lumpen ideologues of caste have emerged, ideologues who refuse to talk of Marx. Marx is anathema for these lumpen ideologues. None of these thinkers could anticipate fascism. None of them could have an original understanding of contemporary Indian reality. To counter liberalism, conservatism and the dictatorship of finance capitalism one needs to start from revolutionary grounds that involve the masses at large. None of these thinkers could allow a philosophical understanding of the masses in revolutionary ferment. And in order to involve the masses at large, one needs the revolutionary humanist method that Marx insisted on especially in his *Economic and Philosophic Manuscripts of 1844*. And just as lumpen ideologues in the service of capitalism and Caste Overlordship emerged, so too emerged the Stalinist bureaucrats in the communist movement. Thus:

> ....the intellectual legacy of Marxism came to be borrowed from sources where, for historical reasons, many of Marx's original works like the *Economic and Philosophic Manuscripts of 1844*, the *Grundrisse* and the *Ethnological Notebooks* would not be available to both the communist ideologues and the cadre. And when these texts became available to the world at large, these never became part of the political repertoire of the Indian Left. In this context the serious analysis of Marxist philosophy, caste and the Asiatic mode of production combined with the idea of multilinear historicism—the alternative subaltern humanist understanding of non-European history—could not be a part of its programme and methodology. This is also because the Indian Left movement from the 1920s was influenced by the Comintern which by 1928 was in total control of Stalin. The theoretical points of references were Stalin's *Dialectical and Historical Materialism*, *Problems of Leninism* and later *Economic Problems of Socialism in the USSR*. It was this Stalinist ideological problematic—half-baked positivism and half crypto-theology—that would be the master-texts for the early communist movement. Communism in India, as general history, is divided into two forms—"communism from below" and "communism from above". That is why I am saying that there are two strands that influenced the early communist movement in India. One was the internal struggles

for democracy in the Indian subcontinent, combined with the heroic struggles of the working classes in Europe, especially the Bolshevik Revolution. But there was another strand, namely what Trotsky called the "Stalin school of falsification". The non-Stalin political strand within the working class movement was almost unknown to the early communists. And when the critique of Stalinism arose, it took the form of a critique of Marxism. M.N. Roy is one such example. In the Stalinist school of falsification the old mythical and theological stories of the conflict of the gods and the devils was rewritten by Stalin as the story of the conflict between the Bolsheviks and the Mensheviks, where the "Party of Lenin" led by the saintly Stalin destroyed the devilish Trotskyites. See J.V. Stalin, G.E. Zinoviev, L. Kamenev, *Leninism or Trotskyism* (Chicago: Daily Worker Publishing Co. 1925). Zinoviev and Kamenev would later be classified as Trotskyites and enemies of the Soviet Union and executed in the infamous Moscow Trials of 1936. The Moscow Trials (1936-38) has been the greatest frame-up known in history. The entire Central Committee of the Bolsheviks at the time of the 1917 Revolution was exterminated by Stalin. Stalin was not only the only member left. He was also the main member who opposed the 1917 Revolution. While Zinoviev and Kamenev's opposition to the 1917 insurrection is known and documented, Stalin's fear of not only the 1917 Revolution, but fear of all revolutions is not yet studied. Stalin killed probably more communists than the fascists. That is why it is important to note the essential features of "counterrevolution from outside" and the "counterrevolution from within".[114]

If the Indian ruling elites inherited caste as schizophrenic racism and the entire colonial system of administration, the Ir.dian Left inherited schizophrenic politics where Marx's humanism was married to Stalinist despotism. Of course such a marriage was impossible and thus a doomed marriage. Despotism would devour Marx's humanism. And since for Stalin the idea of the Oriental despot did not merely signify the Asiatic state or the figure of Timur, but implied Stalin himself, the erasure of the idea of the Asiatic mode of production was essential for Stalin and the Stalinists. One should understand that the Asiatic mode of production is also central to the understanding of Russian society. It is in these perspectives of the Asiatic mode of production with its oversize bureaucracy and the political economy of underdevelopment and dependency to capitalism of the "centre" of global capital accumulation that we shall be able to contextualize not only Indian capitalism and the caste question, but also other forms of non-Westernized capitalism. What one must also say that caste, in form of the clan system, also appears in other societies and this form was also prevalent in Russia which helped the rise of Stalinism. And that is why it is important to see that *caste must not be understood as a mere pre-capitalist remnant, but an active part of capital accumulation in India and other parts of the world.* It is in this context of the global capital accumulation between the centre (West Europe, North America, Japan, etc.) and the periphery (Africa, large parts of Asia and Latin America) that reproduces caste whereby we understand the extremely important and scientific statement that the Indian working classes have two enemies: the culture and ideology of Caste Overlordship (that is realized as the divided self manifested as cultural schizophrenia which produces economic and cultural stagnation) and capitalism.[115] Indian capitalism is not without its ritualistic, hierarchical and bureaucratic flesh that is rotting with its caste-based odour. Note from the quote from the *Rg Veda* how the upper-caste elites—the Brahman Overlords as the producers of ideology—constitute the "hereditary ruling class".[116] The caste elites are thus literally the "mouth" of Indian politics and the ideologues of neoliberal capitalism. Since the ideology of Caste Overlordhip stays dominant even today in the era of twenty-first century late capitalism, it is important to have a look at this very strange ideology and operation. Any application of the European model of transformation of feudalism to capitalism will not work in India.

Caste Overlordship with its hierarchical system manages the caste system. But what is the meaning of Caste Overlordship? By Caste Overlordship as the fetish for ranking, hierarchy and bureaucratic stagnation, one means as Ambedkar says, "the negation of the spirit of liberty, equality and fraternity. In that sense", as he continues, "it is rampant in all classes and is not confined to the Brahmans alone though they have been the originators of it."[117] There is a fetish character involved in this system, since even the oppressed instead of opposing the oppressors became a happy part of it. This system is lethal for even those happy in the unhappy home of this Overlordship. Because of the neurotic and fetish character of this system, everyone wants to be part of it; in fact everyone wants to become this Overlord himself.

Consequently:

> If one puts the caste system in the Marxist perspective, the first three castes comprise various sections of the bourgeoisie, while the last is the Indian working class. Capital, landed property and the wages system, along with state power would be ordered according to caste hierarchy and caste alliances. But a simple reduction of the caste system into the modern class may not exactly be a scientific idea. The relation is mediated by a very complex dialectic. What happens in India is that not only is the upper-caste elite struck by this uncanny caste-clan system, but also the modern proletariat is afflicted by this system which inhibits the formation of a vanguard proletariat (the celebrated *"for itself" proletariat* that Marx talks of in *The Poverty of Philosophy* in his typical Hegelese) that becomes a revolutionary force. And because of the principle of graded inequality, the various sub-castes in the last caste also fight amongst themselves for a superior status, instead of battling directly with the ruling elite. Caste also inculcates a sense of neurosis-psychosis. It is the Indian fascists who recognize caste as neurosis-psychosis and mobilize this for their violent politics. The radical idea of the *annihilation of caste* was turned by them in the ideology of the *perfection of caste*. These issues neither liberal secularism nor the dominant trend in the Indian Left that has been seduced by Stalinism has ever recognized.[118]

Recently after receiving a threat from the liberal Telugu Desanı Party member, Kancha Illaiah Shepherd recalled an article published in the *Economic & Political Weekly* where 46 per cent of corporate board members in the country are said to be Banias, while around 44 per cent are Brahmans.[119] This hegemony has to be understood as absolute control of the Caste Overlords. And this absolute control is in the era of capitalism with its apparatus of Constitutional Democracy and parliamentary democracy.

And because Gandhi and Nehru romanticized caste and because the "race question" that was central to the Indian right-wing from Savarkar to Golwalkar was also taken by Nehru, a truly democratic system could not evolve in India. Democracy was only political. Socially there was (and yet is) hidden apartheid. This apartheid, this sense of superiority, is very strong even today, based on the fallacious ideology of racial descent. The upper castes believe that they descend from "noble races" and from "higher stock".

Note Nehru's *Discovery of India* where the idea of race comes in.[120] He says that caste was in actuality a "peaceful solution" to the conflict between the Aryan and Dravidian races.[121] Yes, it is true that Nehru's sensibilities could never be matched by the Indian right-wing. The problem is that because of his liberal outlook a radical examination and a consequent radical solution could not be given by him or the Congress. He says that "the feudal landlords and their kind who came from England to rule over India had the landlord's view of the world. To them India", so he continues, "was a vast estate belonging to the East India Company, and the landlord was the best and the natural representative of his estate and his tenants."[122] But he did not say that the New Landlords after independence would be both members of the Congress Party and their supporters, both political and financial. He also does not talk of how Gandhi mediated between the landlords and the tenants when the latter rebelled. He does not say that the Indian landlords and capitalists would form the New East India Company.

Further, Nehru mentions Savarkar in high esteem with reference to his writing on the 1857 anti-British revolution.[123] Though critical of both Hindu and Muslim communalism, he does not offer a radical critique of communal-fascism. He is outraged by the "race mania and lynching mentality" that the British exhibited to crush the 1857 mass uprising. But this seems strange that in present-day India, it is the followers of Savarkar and his ideology of Hindutva who are involved in the mass lynching of Muslims. Likewise, he while being critical of the ideology of Hindutva purported by the Hindu Mahasabha, did not critique Madan Mohan Malaviya or "Pandit" and "Malaviyaji" (1861-1946)—twice president of the Congress Party—as he called this early ideologist and leader of the right-wing Hindu Mahasabha.[124] Also for Nehru:

> So long as he (Malaviya) had been one of the leading spirits, the Mahasabha, in spite of its communalism, had not been politically reactionary.[125]

What does it mean? It means that Nehru wanted communalism without being politically reactionary. Likewise he wanted caste without it being politically dangerous. Since we follow the line of thinking that caste has to be understood as a Hegelian *Wesen* (essence), we also claim that this essence continuously grew and from this terrible essence also grew communal-fascism in India. Without caste, fascism in India can never be understood. While Nehru would be critical of fascism and would stand for liberalism, he would only understand fascism at the level of mere appearance. The essence would be left out altogether. It is the Indian fascists who understood caste and how it could be managed and manipulated for achieving total dictatorship.

While Gandhi took on the role of the Overlord, and after him Nehru followed by his daughter Indira Gandhi and her son Rajiv Gandhi, the Congress Party and its social and cultural hegemony remained till the early 1990s. But when finance capitalism wanted to change the entire geo-political map of the world, when Reganomics replaced Roosevelt's New Deal and when socialism would soon be a curse word with the crashing of the Soviet Union; in India to suit the changing portfolio of global capital accumulation, it was right-wing wrath manufactured that would sweep the Congress Party out of power. This new manufacturing of India ideology would have Gandhi's idea of India supplemented with the fascist idea of the war between Hindus and Muslims. The groundwork of fascism was to be made. It was made. Caste with its sense of ranking and superiority would now manufacture hatred against Muslims. And with global Islamophobia, this consent would be a blessed consent.

The Congress could not (and even now cannot) struggle against fascism. To understand this, let us have a look at the following:

> It must be noted that the Indian fascists place at the centre of their violent ideology, the figure of the warrior-priest. But did Indian liberalism not have this image? Did Jawaharlal Nehru and M.K. Gandhi not believe in this warrior-priest ideology? It must also be noted that it is not merely the case that the Indian fascists borrowed (and continue borrowing) from the Nazis. What is interesting to note is that the Nazis were avid readers of the *Vedas* and the *Gita*. And considering that the *Gita*, as the

so-called 'Holy Book' of Hinduism, is being propelled by the RSS to be the National Book, it also implies that the Democratic Constitution is in the process of being sidelined. It must be noted that Heinrich Himmler imagined that he was the mythical Hindu 'hero' Arjun and Hitler was Krishna, the ideologist par excellence of the caste system. For Himmler deeds of the most violent type do not harm the inner self. This he learnt from the *Gita*. Note also how Mathias Tietke the German author of *Yoga in the Third Reich: Concepts, Contrasts, Consequences* talks of how Himmler lectured on reaching the status of "Kshatriyakaste" (the military and ruling elite of ancient India) where salvation (Moksha) is realized through bloody wars. Note also that for Walter Wust—German Orientalist and Nazi ideologue who from 1937 was the President of the Research Institute of the Ahnenerbe (literally "inherited from the forefathers") — Hitler was a "Chakravartin" (Indo-Aryan world emperor). In his speech of Posener, Himmler—influenced by the spirit of the *Gita* where Krishna, the hero of Hindu religion instructs Arjuna to attack his kin and kill them—said that it was the duty of every associate of the SS to carry out action without pity and without considering any human relationships. In this age of mass yoga, which the contemporary Indian fascist government is promoting, it is important to note how yoga enthusiasts like the German Indologist and SS Capt. Jakob Wilhelm Hauer influenced the Nazis on the Aryan theory of racial superiority. The Nazi order according to Himmler was conceived as a spiritual order—a spirituality that led to the consciousness of the superman—willing to kill without looking at the consequences, killing of relatives and family members not excluded. He demanded that one has to detach oneself from such concepts as "good" and "evil." Moksha is this fascist going beyond good and evil. Without this understanding, it is impossible to understand the rise of Indian fascism. Why do we say this? We say this because the Indian bourgeois democratic revolution has not been accomplished and can never be accomplished. In this sense the very idea of the bourgeois democratic revolution could be a myth. This is because the bourgeoisie was incapable of being revolutionary any more. In India the bourgeoisie (especially the bania capitalists, the Kshatriya kulaks and upper caste ideologues, along with the political kulaks and the bureaucracy) carried caste within its economic base and ideological cranium.[126]

And that is why I talk of the re-awakening of the idea of the spectre in the age of triumphant fascism, to be precise the spectre of communism to be able to fight the reality of capitalism, imperialism and fascism. In contrast to this haunting and taunting Red Spectre, we have fascism producing "the traditions of all the dead generations (which) weigh) like a nightmare on the brains of the living".[127] And what do these extreme weighty traditions do? They align with:

> ....a whole series of inherited evils (that) oppress us, arising from the passive survival of antiquated modes of production, with their inevitable train of social and political anachronisms.[128]

They consequently scream:

> We suffer not only from the living, but from the dead. *Le mort saist le vif!* We are seized by the dead![129]

The problem with a society weighed by the caste-past is that it can only and solely live with the dead. Not only was Gandhi a necromantic nationalist who wanted the whole of India to live with the dead, but the entire liberal culture that was constructed became a type of necromantic nationalism. What Indian liberalism did was that it "conjure(d) up the spirits of the past",[130] dressed in "time-honoured disguise", speaking in "borrowed language".[131] It is this borrowed language that one needs to radically critique. What then is this borrowed language of liberalism and how can one critique it?

In Search of a New Ontology

B.R. Ambedkar in his *Who Were the Shudras?* said that:

> It may well turn out that this attempt of mine is only an illustration of the proverbial fool rushing in where the angels fear to tread. But I take refuge in the belief that even the fool has a duty to perform, namely, to do his bit if the angel has gone to sleep or is unwilling to proclaim the truth.[132]

Unlike the liberals led by Gandhi and Nehru, it was B.R. Ambedkar an intellectual unsurpassed in modern India who would offer a radical alternative. The alternative was for the annihilation of the caste system itself. In 1936 when Ambedkar was invited by the Jat-Pat-Todak Mandal to deliver a lecture in

Lahore, he wrote his celebrated *Annihilation of Caste*. This lecture was considered to be too radical and Ambedkar consequently was not allowed deliver it. Nevertheless this radical text remains for posterity to intellectually and politically delve on.

For certain reasons, Indian Marxism has not studied Ambedkar really seriously. Obsessed with the idea of class struggle, they removed any and every reference to social systems that came in the way of class struggle. On the other hand, Ambedkar was seriously challenged by the Congress led by Gandhi and his demands would always be converted into forms of reformism that the Congress would claim to address. Theoretically it would be the theories of Gandhi and Nehru on caste which would prevail and Ambedkar would be left on the periphery of the Indian national movement. The Congress put up other Dalit leaders to counter him during his lifetime, and after his death, the Dalit movement would be totally hijacked by the Congress Party. The idea of the *management of caste* would replace the idea of the *annihilation of caste*. The battle had to be fought in the realm of not only ideas, but the "Idea" itself—the "Idea" of caste.

This "Idea" as the "Idea of the annihilation of caste" had to be explored. What is necessary to be said is that one would not have merely to study Ambedkar seriously, but to create a new paradigm called "Ambedkar Studies". Ambedkar Studies thus has to cover a very large area of research, an area that is unfortunately not explored in detail. This is because the angels (that Ambedkar refers to) have gone to sleep and philosophers are made to look like fools. Nevertheless besides fools and angels, there also exists the revolutionary multitude which is interested in an alternative to the roaming, haunting and taunting ghosts. One thus proceeds to explore this very large area of Ambedkar Studies that still remains concealed. This very large area covers philosophy, political economy, sociology, anthropology, ethnography, jurisprudence, studies in comparative religions, Indo-Iranian Studies, etc. Any scientific study of Ambedkar would have to learn from Marxism and the manner in which Marxist Studies internationally have been involved in the study of the works of Marx and Engels. The *Marx-Engels Gesamtausgabe* or the *Collected Works of Marx and Engels* started by David Riazanov in the 1920s in Moscow and now carried out at the International Institute of Social History in Amsterdam is an example of how research ought to be done.

Because of upper caste hegemony, both in the realm of politics as also in the realm of the social sciences, Ambedkarism has been *captive to a false epistemology*, similar to Marxism that has been captive of a same time of falsity after the advent of Stalin on the scene of history. What is needed is a consequent attempt to free oneself from this *false epistemology* and thus an attempt to create the science of "Ambedkarism", a science that is grounded in a rigorous dialectical materialist methodology. This need is acute, since the post-Ambedkar Ambedkarites with all their aversion to the politics of Hindutva and the attempt to make India into a "Hindu Nation" and the Indian Left will all its hatred for fascism would (because of their false epistemologies) not be able to confront fascism. After all, one could ask the post-Ambedkar Ambedkarites (some are with the Congress, some with the BJP and other parties), that when Ambedkar had said that "if Hindu Raj does become a fact, it will, no doubt be the greatest calamity for this country, Hindu Raj must be prevented at any cost"[133], then why are the followers of Ambedkar so meek in not openly struggling against this type of fascist politics which is imposed on the masses in such a terrible manner?

The answer could be simple. There is a crisis, some would say a political one, and others would say that it is a moral one. But the fact that there is a deep seated crisis which has to be found in theory itself is not seen by many. And just at Lenin reading Hegel in the midst of the First Imperialist World War said that we have Marxists who have not understood Marx[134], so now we say that we have both Marxists devoid of Marx and Ambedkarites devoid of Ambedkar. Both the Indian Left and Ambedkar work in the realm of false epistemology.

One type of this false epistemology—or "false consciousness" (to borrow a term from Engels)[135]—is a consciously created false epistemology, a falsity created by the upper caste elites of the Congress in the first five decades of the twentieth century. This false epistemology initiated by Tilak (as we are saying in this work) was led by Gandhi. But it was not merely Gandhi (and some will say also Nehru, as one finds after reading Perry Anderson's *The Indian Ideology*) that created this false epistemology. The Indian Left led by S.A. Dange also could not understand the epistemic nuances of Ambedkar's thoughts. It then fell prey to Stalinism that created the unilinear theory of history, where caste was located as a mere pre-capitalist formation destined to be destroyed by the inexorable laws of history, once pre-capitalism was destroyed. This rather bizarre theory also suggested that it would be capitalism that would lay the grave of caste. The Indian bourgeoisie were then seen as the revolutionary gravediggers of caste. But capitalism came and caste refused to wither away. Caste thus had to be seen in a different light.

But what then is this different light that could illuminate us on the caste question? What I shall be saying is that caste is seen in a larger ontological space that we know from Marx's writings as the Asiatic mode of production. It is thus to this New Ontology that we need to turn to. But it is not merely the idea of the Asiatic mode of production seen in some sort of economist sense that could throw light on the caste question. It would also be Freudian psychoanalysis that would help us in this perspective. In this sense it could quite be possible—following my *Why We Are Not Hindus*—to attempt constructing the discourse of "Freudo-Marxist Ambedkarism" in order to understand the caste question and then annihilate it (first philosophically) and then actually. For it is in this annihilation of caste—philosophical and actual—that the revolutionary subject would emerge in India. This emergence could possibly lead to the confrontation with fascism and capitalism, both at the same time. The struggles have to be unified struggles. And unified struggles need unified subjects. Mere seeking "subject positions" (to borrow a term of Ernesto Laclau and Chantal Mouffe[136]) will not do.

What we are doing is involving a dialectical materialist and humanist and historicist understanding of Ambedkar. To fight against fascism what I shall be doing to Ambedkar Studies is what Antonio Gramsci did to Marxism. It must be understood that Ambedkar cannot be understood as merely an expert on Constitutional Democracy and a mere student of John Dewey who was transforming the wisdom situated in the archives of Columbia University (it is there that he studied under Dewey) onto India. Nor is he to be seen indebted to the scholarly debt of Edwin Seligman and Alexander Goldenweiser, most certainly not Sidney Webb. He was most certainly not a liberal. Instead I read Ambedkar as a revolutionary and say that just as Marx opened a "continent of knowledge" (as Louis Athusser said in *Lenin and Philosophy* about Marx)[137], so too Ambedkar opens a continent of knowledge. This new continent of knowledge contains the Marxist levels of the economic base and the political and ideological superstructure. Marx's critique of estrangement and Freud's theory of the unconscious repressed are involved in the discovery of this new continent of knowledge.

The idea that Ambedkar was anti-Marxist and that his view of caste was diametrically opposed to Marx's views of class has to be critiqued. Christophe Jafferlot says that in the objectives of the Independent Labour Party started by Ambedkar on August 15, 1936 the word "caste" was mentioned only once.[138] In 1940 he endowed the party with a red flag with eleven stars indicating the eleven provinces of British India.[139] In 1938 he said:

> Really seen, there are only two castes in the world—the first, that of the rich, and the second, that of the poor.[140]

One thus has to free Ambedkarism from the Ambedkarites, just as one has to free Marx from the Marxists. Just as Marx had once said, "All I know is that I am not a Marxist",[141] so too one has to say, "All I know is that I am not an Ambedkarite".

Freed from all dogmas and doctrines, Ambedkarism like Marxism has to be combative. It is then that both can shed their reformist characteristics. It has to strike at the Ideological State Apparatus of the elites. Thus to strike at the Ideological State Apparatus, one needs to articulate how this Ideological State Apparatus produces not only the "hysterical melancholia" (the ideology of Gandhi and Nehru) that I had made central to my understanding of cultural politics in India in my *Why We Are Not Hindus*, but produces now what I call after Fredric Jameson as the "hysterical sublime".[142] The latter is the ideology of Hindutva.

It was Gandhi following the Orientalists who had placed a certain kind of sublime to Hinduism, but a certain kind of melancholia governed this sublime. The Hindu religion was sublime and so were the priests and ideologists of Hinduism sublime. Consider Gandhi:

> Brahmanism owes its unrivalled position to its self-abnegation, its inward purity, its severe austerity—all these illumined by knowledge.[143]

The Gandhian sublime had to reach an ideal world. For Gandhi, "my national service is part of my training for freeing my soul from the bondage of flesh."[144] The freedom movement was merely a means for Gandhi to obtain *moksha*. Gandhi said that he did not think that he was a prophet.[145] Yet it is the mantle of the "Mahatma" that he took with great ease. Said to be an apostle of peace and Hindu-Muslim fraternity his views on Muslims were not exactly encouraging:

> The Mussulman being generally in a minority has as a class developed into a bully.....(where) thirteen thousand years of imperialistic expansion has made the Mussulmans fighters as a body. They are therefore aggressive. Bullying is the natural excrescence of an aggressive spirit.[146]

According to Gandhi, Hinduism is antithetical to the violent bullying characters of the Muslims:

> The Hindu has an ages-old civilization. He is essentially non-violent. His civilization has passed through the experiences that the two recent ones are still passing through. If Hinduism was ever imperialistic in the modern sense of the term, it has outlived its imperialism and has either deliberately or as a matter of course given it up. Pre-dominance of the non-violent spirit has restricted the use of arms to a small minority which must always be subordinate to a civil power highly spiritual, learned and selfless. The Hindus as a body are therefore not equipped for fighting. But not having retained their spiritual training, they have forgotten the use of an effective substitute for arms, and not knowing their use nor having an aptitude for them, they have become docile to the point of timidity or cowardice. This vice is therefore a natural excrescence of gentleness. Holding this view, I do not think that the Hindu exclusiveness, bad as it undoubtedly is, has much to do with the Hindu timidity. Hence also my disbelief in *akhadas* as a means of self-defence. I prize them for physical culture but, for self-defence, I would restore the spiritual culture. The best and most lasting self-defence is self-purification.[147]

While the Congress (following the Orientalists), since the late nineteenth century was actively involved in the creation of the "imagined community" of the "Hindus", little did they think that this "imagined community" of the "Hindus" would cease to be part of the Gandhi-Nehru invention and would join hands with the Indian fascists. This cultural and political production of the imagined community (initially in the Gandhi-Nehru era) veiled the caste structure of society and then repackaged the ideology of graded inequality into a form of natural-spiritual order. But this repackaging now done in the age of late imperialism in permanent crises is causing this hysterical sublime to create fascist mob consciousness where the ideology of riots and wars replaces reason, logic and morality. *The hysterical sublime not only crushes all desire for revolution. It crushes all desire for any form of democracy. There is no reasoning here. What Lukács called the "destruction of reason" would now be complete.*

A study of the dialectical materialist genealogy of the hysterical sublime is necessary to see how hysterical melancholia is transformed into the hysterical sublime. In this "post-truth" age that claims that Gandhi was involved in the creation of a pacifist society where Hinduism was stated to be different from the said violence of Hindutva, it is necessary to dissolve this myth. *Hinduism is Hindutva unarmed and Hindutva is armed Hinduism.* What differentiates them is the difference between the hysterical melancholia and the hysterical sublime. Here it is also necessary to state that this sublime also goes beyond the rationale of Immanuel Kant's idea of the sublime in his *Critique of Judgment*.

It is there that I state that it was Gandhi who was involved in the production of the hysterical melancholia. Hinduism for him (which he intended to preserve at all cost) was about melancholia. But then melancholia, as Walter Benjamin had shown, led to German fascism. Gandhi however linked this form of melancholia with the element of hysteria. His hysteria was however controlled. When Ambedkar called for separate electorates for Dalits (the former "Untouchables"), Gandhi went on one of his innumerable (one can say "infinite" and "imaginary") fasts-onto-death. *There was however no death. Gandhi created this illusion of death. This illusion was grounded in the theme of melancholia.* What is now being produced in the age of triumphant Hindutva is the hysterical sublime. *The transformation of the hysterical melancholia (the imaginary "Hinduism" of Gandhi) into the hysterical sublime (the political Hinduism of the Hindutva school) is the main object of scientific study.*

The question that one may however ask: What is this hysterical sublime and what does this exactly mean? To understand this one turns to Fredric Jameson's *Postmodernism or the Cultural*

Logic of Late Capitalism. According to him, the hysterical sublime is "the experience bordering on terror, the fitful glimpse, in astonishment, stupor and awe of what was so enormous as to crush life altogether".[148] But it is also "the limit of figuration and the incapacity of the human mind to give representation".[149] It is this incapability of giving representation that we need to understand. One also has to understand that the hysterical sublime is basically what Fredric Jameson calls a "phantasmatic relationship with some organic pre-capitalist peasant landscape and village society".[150] So what is this phantasmatic relation with some pre-capitalist imaginary past but caste? In this longing for pre-capitalism, there is not mere nostalgia, there is melancholy. Gandhi's melancholia was happy with this pre-capitalist imaginary past. *The hysterical sublime shows its extreme unhappiness, then converts this unhappiness into rage and this rage into sadomasochistic pleasure.* This hysterical sublime in the age of late imperialism is then understood as creating mass hysteria which serves as the master signifier of the Indian culture industry where people who are unhappy in the unhappy home of capitalism are served with this sense of false happiness. One is not merely happy, but extremely happy in this state of false happiness, where one feels at ease and getting strength from this tragic condition.[151] It is thus both happiness in the state of false happiness and alienation, as also the celebration of this false happiness and alienation. But there is also something else. Consider Jameson:

> The last few years have been marked by an inverted millenarianism in which premonitions of the future, catastrophic or redemptive, have been replaced by senses of the end of this or that (the end of ideology, art, or social class; the "crisis" of Leninism, social democracy, or the welfare state, etc., etc.); taken together, all these perhaps constitute what is increasingly called postmodernism. The case for its existence depends on the hypothesis of some radical break or coupure, generally traced back to the end of the 1950s or the early 1960s.[152]

Further:

> In a classic work, *The Image of the City*, Kevin Lynch taught us that the alienated city is above all a space in which people are unable to map (in their minds) either their own positions or

> the urban totality in which they find themselves: grids such as those of Jersey City, in which none of the traditional markers (monuments, nodes, natural boundaries, built perspectives) obtain, are the most obvious examples. Disalienation in the traditional city, then, involves the practical reconquest of a sense of place and the construction or reconstruction of an articulated ensemble which can be retained in memory and which the individual subject can map and remap along the moments of mobile, alternative trajectories. Lynch's own work is limited by the deliberate restriction of his topic to the problems of city form as such; yet it becomes extraordinarily suggestive when projected outwards onto some of the larger national and global spaces we have touched on here. Nor should it be too hastily assumed that his model—while it clearly raises very central issues of representation as such—is in any way easily vitiated by the conventional poststructural critiques of the "ideology of representation" or mimesis. The cognitive map is not exactly mimetic in that older sense; indeed, the theoretical issues it poses allow us to renew the analysis of representation on a higher and much more complex level. There is, for one thing, a most interesting convergence between the empirical problems studied by Lynch in terms of city space and the great Althusserian (and Lacanian) redefinition of ideology as "the representation of the subject's Imaginary relationship to his or her Real conditions of existence." Surely this is exactly what the cognitive map is called upon to do in the narrower framework of daily life in the physical city: to enable a situational representation on the part of the individual subject to that vaster and properly unrepresentable totality which is the ensemble of society's structures as a whole.[153]

I started with the idea of "false epistemology". I then moved to the idea of "false happiness". In this realm of false happiness, it seems as if not only do we feel at ease at being a "Hindu", but we feel at ease at being a member of the prison-house of caste. And where best can this prison-house of caste be understood? It can be best understood in the 10th Mandala of the *Rg Veda* where the slaughter of primeval "man" is located, the slaughter that gives birth to the uncanny system of caste. The problem with this "false epistemology" is that there was almost no original thinking and if Marx was ever referred, this was subservient to Stalin's manipulation of Marxism. The greatest problem for the Indian

Left (as I shall repeat ad infinitum) is that the idea of the Asiatic mode of production was almost unknown to the early Indian comrades. One must note that it was only E.M.S. Namboodiripad who once used this, only to have this left in the chambers of forgotten reason. Stalin, it must be noted, had literally banned the debate on the Asiatic mode of production. The reason was that it was considered that the Soviet Union under Stalin had nothing to do with socialism and everything to do with this Asiatic mode. Marx's "Oriental despot" (one essential part of this mode of production) would be found in the character of Stalin. The unfortunate fact is that the Indian Left has not yet recognized this. Marx's *Ethnological Notebooks* (published in the early 1970s) by Lawrence Krader would till date be unread by almost all Marxists. As I said earlier, Habib quite recently said that this text is not available to him.[154] In this sense, it seems to be strange that one wants to theorize on the Marxist idea of Indian history when a substantial text of Marx is unread.

In this sense, the understandings of the contemporary mode of production and the revolutionary classes along with the complex-intermixture of modern classes and the caste system was left almost untouched despite the mode of production debate that emerged in the late 1960s. There are many reasons for this. One is the reliance on the Third International which got totally controlled by the Stalinist bureaucrats who wanted to manipulate world revolutions for their own cunning goals. But the main reason for all these anomalies is that after Lenin's death in 1924 a type of theoretical crisis set into the world communist movement whereby Marxist revolutionary repertoire was replaced by what one can call a duplicate Marxism in the form of Stalinism, where the science of revolution was displaced at best for ideologies of managing and manipulating revolution. Stalinism in the early years served as the "manager of the revolution". In actuality it realized itself as the "manager of the counterrevolution". The post-Stalin Stalinists imagined that they were participating in the world revolution. In actuality they were marching hand in hand with the counterrevolutionaries.

Repeating History

Despite the schizophrenic model that the *Rg Veda* prescribes for, if not all humanity, then at least for one part of humanity—

someone is the mouth, someone is something else—and despite this being governed by a form of tragicomedy, there seems to be a form of joy embedded in history that transcends both tragedy and comedy. It was Karl Marx who had said somewhere, and we know where, that according to Hegel, great personalities and events in history repeat itself as it were twice, "he forgot to add" as Marx says, "the first time as tragedy, the second as farce".[155] Marx, it seems, should have said that history repeats itself thrice, the third time as great joy. In a certain sense we are sitting on the crossroads of history where tragedy, farce and joy appear all at the same time.

Keeping this theme of repeating history we turn to the problem of identifying caste in India, especially in identifying the genealogy of caste. Tragedy shall be inexorably linked to the genealogy of caste. Central to this theme of caste is the question of capitalism and modern classes and whether the new capitalist structures are able to erase the earlier caste-based mode of discrimination. If tragedy is linked to the genealogy of caste, farce is related to the question of the persistence of caste in the age of modernity. The joy that we are all waiting for is the joy that is waiting in the wings of revolutionary history.

To herald this revolutionary joy one must study the relation between social hierarchies and graded inequality, the sine qua non of the caste system, and the Marxist idea of class struggle After all, one may ask: Why does Indian society have a hierarchical structure based on purity and pollution (similar to the white/black divide in the USA and Europe) and why is there a great pleasure derived by the ruling elites in celebrating these hierarchies? And why is violence against Dalits present in Indian society even decades after accepting the Constitution? Are these forms of continuous violence similar to the racial forms of violence found in various parts of the world? We thus state that caste is not equal to race, but casteism is a form of racism, albeit a form of *schizophrenic racism* where we are able to keep these four problems of caste as:

1. estranged clannishness,
2. class,
3. South Asian form of race and racism as schizophrenic racism, and
4. neurosis and psychosis.

Since I am stating that caste is a form of schizophrenic racism and caste violence is a form of racist violence, one must recall however that Ambedkar was of the view that caste is not akin to race and that diverse types of people form the contours of the Indian subcontinent. At surface level this idea of Ambedkar who said that caste is not race seems to differ from that of Jyotiba (Jotirao) Phule who observed that caste and the problem of "race" coincided. Phule talked of the entire discourse of "Hinduism" as a form of colonialism where the Brahmans as the leaders of the Indo-Iranian warrior-priests raided and occupied in the Indian subcontinent. In actuality I see the synchronization of this thesis with that of Ambedkar. The historical periods in the Phulean and Ambedkaritean arguments are different.

For Phule the Brahmans were part of the "horde of the Aryans from Iran"[156] that colonized India (for Phule India is "the land of Bali"). For Ambedkar, however one cannot talk of people from a particular caste being descents of a particular "race".[157] One must thus state that race and racism are not the same. In fact one can also state that there is nothing called "race". *What one can say is that there is nothing called "race", yet there is something called racism.* That is why I am saying that though caste is not race, castism is racism and I am saying that this form of racism is *schizophrenic racism*. To recall Ambedkar, "some have dug a biological trench in defence of the caste system".[158] What is important to understand is that the "caste system does not demarcate racial division".[159] Yet "an immense lot of nonsense is talked about hereditary and eugenics in defence of the caste system".[160]

What happened is that the caste elites with the help of the nineteenth century fashionable ideology of eugenics imagined that caste is akin to race and they (the Brahmans) are nothing but the original Europeans. Savarkar and Golwalkar were strong supporters of the "race question". For them the Aryans (read: "upper caste Hindus") were of one race in a mythical battle with the Semitic race (read: "Muslims"). In the colonial era, the caste system was refashioned with the help of colonial ideology of eugenics and racial superiority. The Indian communal-fascists mastered this colonial ideology.

What happens with twentieth century capitalism in India is that caste violence imitated the type of racial violence practised by the White Supremacists against the Afro-Americans in USA.

By the middle of the twentieth century the cultural, ideological and economical subordination of the Dalits along with the Brahmanical form of stratification and rituality started miming the violence of racism in the USA and Western Europe. The role of the Colonial Census of 1901 headed by Herbert Risley[161] in classifying people according to his rather absurd thesis of "race science" played a disastrous role in the restructuring of caste in the twentieth century. The uneven character of capitalism in India whereby the general law of capital accumulation threw Dalits into the Industrial Reserve Army led not only to the capitalist-proletariat opposition, but also the economic opposition having racial connotations. In the 1970s in Maharashtra the Dalit Panthers were formed, inspired by the Black Panther movement in USA. They linked caste with race.

What I am arguing is that instead of a blanket ahistorical understanding of caste formations in the Indian subcontinent, it is better to have a historical materialist understanding of the same. Thus one needs to ask how the "high" castes: the priests (Brahmans), the warriors (Kshatriyas) and merchants (Vaiśyas) became part of the ruling establishment and the Śūdras and ati-Śūdras became the proletariat and the disenfranchised people of India. One needs, however, to ask whether this neat division was amazingly always present in Indian history or whether Indian history offers another reading of caste where caste equations do continuously change without disturbing the caste order.

Capital has however fashioned caste according to its own image. Caste most certainly is not static.[162] What needs to be recognized is that India's uneven development in capitalist development that grew from the Asiatic mode of production never attempted to annihilate caste. Neither legally, nor in terms of economic development was caste in itself challenged in post-independent India. Instead capitalism has undoubtedly witnessed "the intensity of violence against the Dalits".[163] The last few years has seen how this violence has been transfigured into a cruel and beastly exhibition where through mobile video recording, public spectacles of lynching have been created. Violence against Dalits and Muslims has thus become a spectacle of phantasmagorical levels where violence has been publicly celebrated. For reasons (well known) the Indian state has never penalized these barbaric acts. What we also see that it is not violence against Dalits that has been classified as terrorists acts. Instead we see that Dalit resistance is now being seen as left-wing terrorism deemed to be fit for total annihilation.

Somehow caste and class have a very close symbiotic relationship. Yet what needs to be said as that one cannot collapse the understanding of caste into that of class. Instead one has to talk of a *caste-clan mode of production* as an alternative to the understanding of Indian history that R.S. Sharma and Irfan Habib had earlier offered. Thus what I am saying is that a complete re-hauling of the understanding of Indian history is necessary—a certain kind of decolonizing and revolutionizing of Indian history—where reason could replace the muttering of angry statements. Thus:

> One cannot put the understanding of caste and class in a formal Aristotelian either/or binary. One cannot say: "only class", as the way, by and large the Parliamentary Left has been doing. But one also cannot say: "only caste" as parties based on identity politics do. One has to understand class and caste, as "next door neighbours, and it is only a span that separates the two." The radical difference is that modern classes are fluid and mobile, while the caste system is ossified. India has both these two locked in its unfortunate breast.[164]

That is why it is important to reiterate the specific nature of caste and how as caste-clan, the study of caste has to develop fresh epistemic mechanisms. Caste cannot be reduced to class. But caste cannot avoid class. Instead one must note that class and caste, are "next door neighbours, and it is only a span that separates the two."[165] In this neighbourhood I say that caste gets aligned to class and class to caste and that at both levels of the ideological superstructure and the economic base one has to unleash a cultural revolutionary attack on both the political economy of the caste mode of production as well as its ideological superstructure and justifier called "Hinduism".

What needs to be said is that there is nothing in reality called "Hinduism". Yet "Hinduism" exists. What does this mean? It means that there was a system of religious codes constructed, a system that took mythical form. "Hinduism" thus implies a religious-mythical system and "Hindus" are those that are submerged in this myth. For Ambedkar since this mythical system negated the ideas of liberty, equality and fraternity it took a necessarily tyrannical form. And it is in this attack of reason against tyranny that would be the prelude to the critique of political economy in India. In this perspective of the caste-class combine, one must also note that while caste remains a part of the history of India in particular, caste takes a more generic form where understood as an oppressive social system was also linked to the Asiatic states. Trotsky thus in *The Permanent Revolution & Results and Prospects* and *The Revolution Betrayed* went even so far as to link caste to the counterrevolutionary bureaucratic Stalinist state[166]. It is thus necessary to widen the horizons of caste and link caste as an ossified group with an entrenched closed mentality to the Stalinist bureaucracy.

The wielders of the Ideological State Apparatus of India, are always accompanied by the military elites and the bearers of the Repressive State Apparatus who control the army, the police and the paramilitary forces. What is important to note is that the Ideological State Apparatus is always accompanied with the Repressive State Apparatus. The upper caste ideologues have the warrior-gladiators with them. It is the duty of these gladiators to kill, in fact to kill without thinking, without remorse. Thus in what we know as the imagined discourse of "Hinduism" we have in the "Book" the *Gita* an entire ideologically thought-out repertoire of caste. Consider Hegel here who says that in the Gita:

> ...the first chapter (*padu*), says Colebrook, treats of contemplation, the second the means to reach it, the third treats of the exercise of transcendental power, *Vibhuti*, and the fourth of abstraction or spiritual detachment.[167]

Note all the four steps and note what the warrior mind does in the last step. We have the "persistent direction of the mind towards the Godhead, whereby it withdraws from all other things".[168] The question then posed is: What is this state of withdrawal, none than the withdrawal from all reality that Freud had characterized as the feature of the psychotic? Further: What does the warrior mind that has become psychotic do? It cautions against the "mixture of castes" and the "spurious births".[169] Consequently:

> The negative nature of the most sublime in Indian religiosity is also satisfied with a wholly abstract renunciation, devoid of any state of emotion—the direct killing.[170]

While the warrior caste is created along with the ideology of wars, there are other castes, the peasants and the artisans. Indo-Iranian history is witness to the Great Class Struggle between the two basic classes, the priests and the warriors on one side and the peasants and the artisans on the other side. In India it was the warrior-priests who could first state their hegemony before the advent of Buddhism and Jainism. Then after the downfall of firstly the Maurya Empire (322 B.C.E.–185 B.C.E.) and finally the Kushanas (45 C.E.–73 C.E.) and with the rise of the Gupta Empire (240 to 590 C.E.) followed by Shankara's philosophical exposition of Advaita Vedanta under the Chalukya dynasty of Badami, headed by Vikramaditya II (733–746 CE), caste would get a fresh lease of life. What Hegel calls "lines of demarcation"[171] (a term used then that Lenin keeps central to his *What is to be Done?* followed by Althusser's *Lenin and Philosophy*) now feature in the demarcations of caste boundaries.

In this sense the foundational myth stated in the 10th mandala of the *Rg Veda*—where the Brahmans are said to be to the mouth and speech act of the schizophrenic-stratified god, and other castes-classes said to be arms, thighs and feet and also many things besides that are totally alienated from the sacred Brahmanical mouth—stands even today as the reality of the social and political life-world of so-called "modern" India. This reality of caste is both an awful actuality as well as an ideology of ages gone by. Since it is of a past and dying ideology we call it a ghost. Just as Hamlet was haunted by the ghost of his dead father, so too modern India is haunted by the ghost of Hindu religion. But this ghost is no mere ghost—albeit a haunting one. It is a traumatic ghost. Caste is thus the trauma of Indian civilization.

Look everywhere in India, we shall find this ghost, the ghost of the Caste Overlord dressed (mostly) in democratic attire. But beneath all this clothing, the fascist body and mind are found. Of course the liberals could never do anything about this ghost and the return of the Overlord. The Left was expected to do something. But it was also left dumb to the teeth. What they did was only create ideologies, sometimes also producing ideologies of revolution, just as the Utopians always promised heaven on earth. And what did these ideologies of revolution (that are not only indifferent to the science of revolution, but which actively repressed this science) do? These ideologies created the framework of an alienated and alien discourse—a form of reified consciousness—whereby the social framework of Indian society and history was actively veiled.

In India the crux of the problem was the inability to identify the nature of the dominant mode of production which itself is based on the inability to understand the mechanism and dynamics of Indian history. What the Indian Left did was that it borrowed the unilinear and mechanist idea of history—where history was said to be a march-past from primitive communism via slave society, feudalism and capitalism, finally destined to culminate in communism. R.S. Sharma's theory of "Indian feudalism" and the Indian Left's idea of the New Democratic Revolution are examples of this mechanistic and unilinear theory of history. That this mechanical understanding governed by what Stalin considered to be "iron laws" reminiscent of theology was something that the Indian Left never bothered to ponder about. And since "iron laws of history" have never made real political revolutions, and since events are always made by real humans, the Communist Party imagined that it would appear as the messianic representation of these laws of history. Stalin (literally meaning the "man of steel", as we noted at the beginning of this work) became the messianic representation of the iron laws of history. History would soon be replaced with messianic tendencies, on the one hand, and contemplation, on the other hand. In the contemporary Left movement, the Maoists represent the messianic tendency, while the Parliamentary Left (that went as the "Left Front") became the contemplative part. What the dominant trend of the Indian Left did not understand is that Stalin left the legacy of the decaffeinated revolution, a revolution which does not smell and taste of a revolution.

This decaffeinated revolution, this imaginary revolution of the Established Indian Left could never involve a critique of the cultural politics of the Indian ruling establishment. Except writing historical treatises, they could never go to the masses, informing them of the false constructs of Indian history and Indian nationhood. Note in contrast, Ambedkar's radical critique where he not only chides the idea of a "Hindu Nation" (now realized in the phantasmagorical form of "Hindu Rashtra"), but critiques the very idea of "Hinduism as being mythical.

How then can the "Hindu Rashtra" ever be possible when we know that "Hindu society is a myth"?[172] Don't people know that "Hindu society as such does not exist"?[173] The pertinent question that one needs to ask is: Why did the Left totally ignore Ambedkar? Why did the Left not unleash an in-depth attack on the entire cultural aspect of India called "Hinduism"? Yes one had Debiprasad Chattopadhyaya making an alleged "materialist" theory of ancient India. But this materialism did not mean Marx's materialism.[174] It was definitely a pre-Marxist materialism. In fact it was not merely pre-Marxist materialism that dominated Marxist theory in India; it was pre-Marxism that determined its very politics. Revolutionary praxis was totally absent from this repertoire. Revolutionary politics would be totally missing from the political repertoire of the Established Left. While the parliamentary comrades would be caught up in the fantasies of liberal democracy, the Maoists would take their mythical guns fighting for a mythical revolution. They did not know that Mao's goal was state capitalism and as he said in his *Critique of Soviet Economics,* Marx's theory of value had to be revised such that value-exchange value-money-capital-classes could all fit in his idea of "socialism with Chinese characteristics".

Since Marxism did not have a revolutionary materialistic problematic, it thus lacked the project of the Enlightenment where humanism and science could be part of the collective imagination. The imagination of the past thus entered. The fact that we are seized by the dead is thus apparent. This lack of the Indian Enlightenment created an *alienated vacuum* whereby fascist forces entered and occupied this space of *alienated vacuum*. Marx's theory of alienation is not restricted to political economy. It is much larger than previously imagined.

Mao thought that he could master how value (and consequently money and capital) could be controlled. The fascists knew that they could control and be controlled by capital much better than either the liberals, Stalinists and Maoists. They knew that they could be the best masters and slaves of capital.

Class Formlessness and Class Duty

Since the project of so-called "hitherto existing socialism" (rather "hitherto non-existing socialism") collapsed in 1991 with the complete dismembering of the Soviet Union, liberalism woke up in a state of wrath. They had to prove that the ideas of class and class struggle are illusions. In India because of caste the illusions of class would become the non-reality of class. Caste as "enclosed class" does not allow class as modern class to be actualized.

The Eighteenth Brumaire of Louis Bonaparte is a good illustration of how from a type of class confusion caused by class formlessness, the leader of the lumpen proletariat appears. In the nineteenth century this leader who pretended to soar above all classes appeared as Louis Bonaparte. In the twentieth century this leader was the fascist superman who appeared in Italy in 1922 and Germany in 1933. This appearance of the fascist superman is based on class confusion and class formlessness. Fascism, one must note, hates classes. Fascism loves the myth of the superman, whether it is the fascism of Mussolini and Hitler, or the Asian fascism of the Ayatollahs and other evangelic theologians. Thus:

> Classes, class struggle and class solidarity are, as we all well know, the basis of Marxist science of historical materialism. The formation of proletarian class formation and class solidarity would need what Marx calls "common existence" and "common interest". In India, this commonness would manifest itself not so much as in proletarian class solidarity, as in the brutal antagonism of caste groups built on monopolistic power, rank worship, the upper caste ideology of "labour as outcaste" and a parasitical-authoritarian bureaucracy completely alienated from the masses. Coupled with this caste-bureaucratic system, would be finance capitalism which would now model this Oligarchic state as the Managerial Corporate State. "An oppressed class", so Marx continues, "is the vital condition for every society founded on the antagonism of classes". But in India this formlessness of class that we are mentioning and the domination of the caste system would propel an uncanny economic system along with the even more uncanny cultural and ideological superstructure the world has ever known. Moksha, so we know from this uncanny course of events, has been reached. But not merely individual moksha, political moksha. What is moksha? Moksha is not merely the release from the cycle of birth and death which the priests, sages and professors of philosophy had taught us. It is not a form of spiritual emancipation. It is going beyond good and evil, a

going beyond that seek the status of the fascist superman. It is also a form of nihilism that Friedrich Nietzsche had recognized as the sickness of contemporary times. Modern India (i.e. after these very strange elections) has achieved this cynical moksha. The fascist supermen have stormed the parliament. According to Hegel, history was to realize itself in the kingdom of reason. In India it would realize itself in fascism. 2014 would be like 1933 in Germany. Behind the posters announcing the era of development would be the fascist swastika. Why did this happen? Why did the Indian elites have to be obsessed with moksha and not with reason? It is not merely because the Indian elites built an entire edifice of political manipulation, economic depravity and cultural cynicism. It is because those who thought that moksha is not only a joke but some form of tragicomedy, those who thought that revolution is an answer to manipulation, depravity and cynicism, would want a decaffeinated revolution, a revolution which does not smell of revolution. But then decaffeinated revolutions could also be forms of counterrevolution. The ugliest face of counterrevolution would manifest itself in the middle of 2014. Why is this so? It is because instead of revolutionary zeal of internationalism and concrete analysis of concrete conditions (methodological themes that were central to Revolutionary Marxism, themes that made the 1917 Bolshevik Revolution), one had the zeal of revolution dampened with the decaffeinated revolution—the revolution that would only be an imagined revolution. This is despite the heroic struggles that the cadres of the various Communist Parties unleashed and despite their presence in large parts of the country especially in the states of Tripura, West Bengal and Kerala, not to forget the Red Corridor that brings in shivers to the Indian bourgeoisie.[175]

So how does "class" come into being from the phantasmagorical formlessness that caste ensures? In Europe the question was of transforming this "class-in-itself" into "class for-itself" whereby a class developed that became conscious of the ontology of labour, conscious that the entire world of social wealth is produced by its own labour, conscious that this wealth is seized by the bourgeoisie and that the edifice of poverty, riots and wars are created henceforth from this capitalist mode of production and thus conscious that revolution is the answer.

The annihilation of caste is inherent in this revolution. There is no other alternative. This annihilator-destroyer of caste is the "*class with radical chains*". It is thus:

> ......a class of civil society which is not a class of civil society, a class [*Stand*] which is a dissolution of all classes, a sphere which has a universal character because of its universal suffering......This dissolution of society as a particular class is the proletariat.[176]

Now it is important to concretely philosophize this idea of the proletariat. On the one hand, the ontology of labour is central to the idea of the proletariat. What is important to note is that we must move away from the reductionist ideas of the proletariat that refuses to see the philosophical side of this question. After all, the question that needs to be posed is: Why does Marx put the proletariat central to his idea of revolution? The answer has to be given in a Hegelian manner. First, one has to grasp the "Idea" of the proletariat. Once one grasps this idea one sees the dialectics of negation in this very "Idea". This dialectics of negation serves as the *active revolutionary force*. It has to be differentiated from the *reactive Stalinist force*. It consequently *sets* the agenda for politics in India. Its philosophy is the *negation of negation*. It thus proclaims what Marx calls the "*dissolution of the hitherto existing world order*" by stating "the *secret of its own existence*, (which is) the dissolution of that world order".[177] Just as Marx once said: "Philosophy cannot be made a reality without the abolition of the proletariat, the proletariat cannot be abolished without philosophy being made a reality",[178] one now says philosophy can be made a reality only with the abolition of caste.

What has happened in India is the retardation of both the class of the proletariat as well as its very "Idea". Here the caste-clan apparatus has not allowed the development of the class of the proletariat to become the universal class, the class whose mission is to dig the graves of capitalism. And when the working class emerged because of industrialization, it had on its backs and minds this same dreadful caste-clan apparatus. Instead we have what Marx in the *Grundrisse* calls "forms which precede capitalist production"[179] dominating capitalism itself. These pre-capitalist forms function as "locality clans"[180] and appear as the:

> ......caste order, in which one is separated from the other, without the right of inter-marriage, quite different in [degree of] privilege; each with an exclusive, irrevocable occupation.[181]

Note that these "locality clans" suppress every form of universality. And since caste excludes the status of the universal class and the dreams of universality any form of democratic transformation of society was and is impossible. The problem with the Indian Left is that they did not view the essentiality of caste as anti-universality, did not see that multi-linearity is essential to Marx's original project, did not see that history does not follow this blind telos from primitive communism, via slave society, feudalism and capitalism, mysteriously evolving into communism driven of course by the messiah. One is waiting for the messianic magic for socialism to enter the stage of history. And since Stalin as Yusuf II and the butchers of the Bolshevik Revolution reigned supreme after Lenin's death, only theoretical confusion ruled the roost. *Class formlessness would be accompanied with theoretical formlessness.*

In contrast to this class formlessness, let us look into the formation of the proletariat as the bearer of world emancipation. In the *Manifesto of the Communist Party* the authors said that "the immediate aim of the Communists is the formation of the proletariat into a class".[182] And this formation into a class leads to the "overthrow of bourgeois supremacy" and the "conquest of political power by the proletariat".[183] This proletariat class tells the bourgeoisie that it is "unfit to be the ruling class in society".[184]

But as Lars Lih has so well demonstrated this formation into a class that overthrows the bourgeoisie has to be understood as a "world historical mission of the workers to take power and to introduce socialism".[185] And it is the "great duty" of the proletariat to carry out its mission.[186] In carrying out its duty it scripts its "world-historical epic".[187] This revolutionary role has to be emphasized. Class formlessness and caste politics always depreciates this revolutionary role. As Marx said:

> To conquer political power has therefore been the great duty of the working classes.[188]

Thus when Lih talks of the "world-historical mission of the workers" he is following Marx who talks of the "great mission of the proletariat".[189] Caste and class formlessness will be the active negation of this revolutionary mission of the proletariat. The duty of the proletariat is to create a world socialist order, that of caste to destroy this order. Consequently:

> It is important to understand that Indian society is a society based on "gradation of castes forming an ascending scale of reverence and a descending scale of contempt", a gradation that has helped the fascists to power. In this case, Indian capitalism has this hierarchical system of lordship and bondage, along with the scale of reverence and contempt, deeply etched in its economic, cultural and ideological cranium. The form of class relations that emerged in India would appear as an "enclosed class" system, even as a "gang or clique". Appearing as "warring groups" and "close corporations", the caste system prevented proletarian class politics to bloom. As the "caste-clan system" and as *clannishness that pervades the dominant economic and political orders,* what bloomed was the not so flowery flower of fascism.

Indian Nationalism and the Problem of Schizophrenic Racism

So how is caste to be broken, considering that it is deeply etched in the Indian mode of production supported by the Patronizing State which instead of critiquing caste, actually rationalized it, by giving it legal status and then took this very apparatus for capitalist governance? Here it must be pointed out that Ambedkar was right when he singled Gandhi and the Congress Party as being responsible for the reproduction of caste, in fact for the active reproduction of caste.

Thus the elites instead of relying on secular principles actively engaged in religion and religious obscurantism and institutionalized these in the public space. Gandhi was chiefly responsible for this. He institutionalized caste with the help of the rising upper caste bourgeoisie who converted caste and religion into commodities. Take the example why the *Gita* which came into prominence, only with the European Orientalists was now made to govern the public space. It is once again to Gandhi that one must point our revolutionary fingers. The *Gita* the text that Ambedkar thought to be a counterrevolutionary text, promoting violence and wars was made not only to enter the public space, but made to govern this very space. After all, why was Gandhi, the alleged apostle of peace and non-violence referring to the *Gita*? Was it because his idea of non-violence was only the *other of violence,* or *latent violence*?

Gandhi's endeavour was not in solitude. He was joined by Jaydayal Goyandka and Hanuman Prasad Podder, two Marwari businessmen who would brand themselves and their new bourgeois production as the "Gita Press". This new commodity would be branded as "spiritualistic". The "Hindu public space" was created. While the Orientalists were producing this "Hinduism" in the space of theoretical ideology, Gandhi and the Marwari business were producing this "Hindu public space" in the space of real politics. The tie up of Orientalism with Gandhism and the Marwari businessmen would turn out to be deadly. What then happened was that a terrible right-wing melody was created where Gandhism was joined by the Marwari bourgeoisie. It was thus logical and easy for the ideology of Madan Mohan Malaviya and the Hindu Sabha to enter the Congress Party.

For mainstream secularists, Gandhi is seen as a secular leader and the Hindutva icons, V.D. Savarkar and M.S. Golwalkar as fascist hate mongers. This type of theorization is false, since it leaves out real history, leaves out the role of Marwari business in the production of this "Hinduness" that formed the basis of political Hinduism. Political Hinduness was not created by the simple hatred of the other (Christian, Muslim). It was created as a modern commodity where the fiction of sanatana Hindu dharma was created with its further fictions of ahimsa and moksha. The creation of the Christian and Muslim as the "hellish other" was concretized by this bania created fiction.

Of course it is not the case that "Muslim communalism" did not exist. It did, and its creation was from the Muslim middle class educated at Aligarh Muslim University. Here it is not the Muslim mullahs who were responsible for the production of Muslim communalism, which led to the tragic partition of the Indian subcontinent and the break-up of the unity of the popular classes. It was the Western educated Muslims led by Syed Ahmed Khan or "Sir Syed" to be precise. Just as Hindu communalism was the creation of the upper caste elites, Muslim communalism was the creation of the Muslim gentry. Here one must note the foundation at Dhaka of the Muslim League, on December 30, 1906 was by the All India Muhammadan Educational Conference, which was the child of Syed Ahmed Khan. After the formation of the Muslim League in 1906 the Punjab Hindu Sabha was established in 1909 by Arya Samaj leaders Lala Lajpat Rai (1865-1928) and Rai Bhadhur

Lal Chand (1852-1912). The Mahasabha was thus established with Madan Mohan Malaviya presiding over the Sabha's first session at Lahore in October of the same year. Since it is thought that the Congress and the Hindu Mahasabha were opposed to one another, it must be noted that in April 1915, the All India Hindu Sabha was formed at the Kumbh Mela in Haridwar, where Gandhi was present at the conference.[190] Neither Gandhi nor the Congress were opposed to the formation of the Hindu Mahasabha. It is necessary to demystify this myth since it has become fashionable in liberal circles to equate the Hindu Mahasabha with Savarkar and then oppose, Gandhi to Savarkar. According to this myth, Gandhi was secular while Savarkar was fascist.

What we are doing is pointing out that the ideas of the "Muslim" and the "Hindu" came to be developed as not merely two religions, followed by two nations, but as different races in perpetual war with one another. In this sense both the leaders of the Muslim League (Syed Ahmed Khan) and the Hindu Mahasabha (particularly Madan Mohan Malaviya), were responsible. While it seems that the Congress was secular and stayed far away from these two trends, as noted above this was not so. Thus while the Hindu Mahasabha after the Muslim League's foundation in 1906 fashioned an "imaginary Hindu community", modelled in exact mirror image of the "imaginary Muslim community", what the Congress did was not debunking this myth of religious communities. What it did was that it took this myth of the two imaginary communities and then merely talked of a mythical brotherhood of these two imaginations.

In the *Indian Express*, Mark Tully thought that Hinduism could be used to counter Hindutva, since it has no dogmas[191]. He recalls R.C. Zaehner to mobilize these views. Tully does not talk of caste and the dharma of caste, does not talk of *varnashramdharma*, the segregation of women and the subaltern castes, untouchability, etc. Quoting from the *Upanishads* and talking of the "spiritual" is like a psychotic Nazi talking of peace at Auschwitz. India needed a cultural revolution. It got Ambedkar, but the Congress with its Hindu Mahasabha interior assured that his views on Hinduism would not be realized in the public space.

What has so far not been imagined is that it was the elites who were involved in this myth making of the imaginary called "Hinduism". The real foundation of India is not religion and thus religious communities, but caste which stands as a counterrevolution on which stands the edifice of contemporary politics. This "spiritualization" in the realm of politics and ideology of the Caste Overlords institutionalized stagnation and the politics and culture of backwardness, dependency and slavery. It seems the elites had not heard of Phule's masterpiece entitled *Slavery*. Or if they did, it had to be forgotten.

A revolution was needed. It had to be a revolution in the realm of ideas. And since the entire space of the nation dominated by the "Hindu imaginary" had colonized the public space, one needed to move away from this space. It is here that we talk of a separate organization of the subaltern people. Democracy of any kind could not be actualized from within the space occupied by the Caste Overlords. For Ambedkar one needed a "separate organization for the Depressed Classes"[192] where a radical shakeup was necessary. For:

> When the bottom-most stone in the structure was shifted from its place, those above it were bound to be shaken out of their positions.[193]

In this respect, as Ambedkar said, "Hindu society must organize on modern lines breaking its age-long framework".[194] For Gandhi (contra Ambedkar) Hinduism is necessary in its most archaic form. For Gandhi, a Hindu has to be a good Hindu, for Ambedkar one had to convert.[195] Gandhi wanted ritualistic religion to govern the public space, Ambedkar wanted a humanist one.[196]

Ambedkar's ideal was fraternity[197] based on what Étienne Balibar calls "equa-liberty". On the other hand:

> Hindu religion does not recognize the principle of equality of social status; on the other hand it fosters inequality by insisting upon grading people as Brahmans, Kshatriyas, Vaishyas and Shudras which now stands towards one another in an ascending scale of hatred and descending scale of contempt.[198]

What needs to be pointed out that these scales of hatred and contempt are racist through and through. Consequently, it is not equality that stands central to India, even modern India, but inequality, in fact graded inequality. And Gandhism as the permanent counterrevolution was responsible for solidifying graded inequality in the modern era. Gandhi was the counterrevolutionary par excellence. He was Manu II. For this modern Manu, the world had to be based on *Dukha* or suffering.

While literature exists which exposes a section of the Indian right-wing as being influenced by Nazism and the race question, the relation of Nazism to Hinduism and Gandhi has not been considered. For the Nazis, the state had to be a racial state based on purity of the blood. Duty, for duty's sake while sounding very ethical is strictly speaking here a post-Kantian phenomenon. In Kant, humanity to be considered as a kingdom of ends is central to ethical imagination; in the post-Kantian (even post-Hegelian and post-Marxist world) duty is fraught with fascist connotations. Note Gandhi on the *Gita*:

> It I were not to perform my task these worlds would be ruined;
> I should be the cause of chaos and of the end of all mankind.[199]

For Gandhi, the working class comprises of "ignorant people" for they work with attachment.[200] Kant's idea of "disinterested pleasure" from his *Critique of Judgment* is transfigured into action that is done "disinterestedly".[201]

Besides his alleged disinterestedly performed action, the leitmotiv of Gandhi's ideology comes up. There should be no "confusions of *varnas* in society".[202] Like Himmler and the Nazi supremacist ideology, the ideal person:

> ....should, therefore, go on doing his duty in the spirit of yoga, unattached to the fruits of his work, and inspire others to do work likewise.[203]

Gandhi's idea of "duty" is "through violence", to be precise "deliverance from the existing body through violence".[204] One would ask: Does Gandhi not sound like a postmodern jihadist? Is not his idea of doing "duty for striving for *moksha*"[205] a jihadist idea where the jihadist mass murders only to attain paradise and the huris? One can then ask Gandhi and the jihadists:

> You say rivers of wine flow in heaven,
> is heaven a tavern to you?
> You say two huris await each believer there,
> is heaven a brothel to you?

But Gandhi's idea of moksha and paradise is devoid of all poetic sensibilities. Consider this:

> You have already committed violence. By talking now like a wise-man, you will not learn non-violence. Having started on this course, you must finish the job.[206]

The danger in Gandhi is that he treats the epic *Mahabharata* not as history, but a a "*dharma grantha*", a text without an "actual event."[207] In this phantasmagoria, the text is written "to explain man's duty in his inner life".[208] Further for Gandhi:

> This is not a battle which took place one thousand years ago: it is one which is raging all the time, even today.[209]

Gandhi transfigures myth to the level of modern psychology:

> Breathing involves killing, which is unavoidable violence and is, therefore forgiven. Without such unavoidable violence we cannot keep alive the body for its sacred pilgrimage.[210]

Unavoidable violence, sacred pilgrimage? What is this? Is this not fascism? What is the essence of fascism, besides being totally brutal, racist and anti-democratic? *The essence of fascism is pseudo-rebellion.* The fascist before grabbing power imagines himself as an anarchist. He imagines that he will abolish the parliament. He considers that the parliament is a sterile woman and prostitute. In this sense this fascist-cum-anarchist is no different from Gandhi's understanding of politics in the *Hind Swaraj*.[211] For this anarchist imagination:

> That which you consider to be the Mother of Parliament is like a sterile woman and a prostitute.......The Parliament has not yet, of its own accord, done a single good thing. Hence I have compared it to a sterile woman. The natural condition of the Parliament is such that, without pressure, it can do nothing. It is like a prostitute because it is under the control of ministers who change from time to time......Parliament is without a real master. Under the Prime Minister, its movement is not steady but it is buffeted about like a prostitute.[212]

Gandhi would not be alone in this ideological rendering. He would be accompanied by both Hitler and Stalin. While Hitler would clearly stand out as a World Despot, Stalin would be the Oriental despot par excellence. No wonder that he obliterated all references to Marx's original idea of the Asiatic mode of production headed by the Oriental despot. The Oriental despot had to be forgotten. It was forgotten. In this forgetfulness the crimes of the despot were written as the crimes of Leninism and Bolshevism.

Why is the Asiatic Despot Forgotten?

The answer is simple. The Oriental despot would not merely be Timur racking the souls without measure. It would be Stalin. But as we have seen Stalin is not alone. We have with him Gandhi. In this part we must restrict ourselves to Stalin. What would be known since February 22, 1956 Twentieth Congress of the CPSU as the "cult of the individual" would be directly related to the question of the Asiatic mode of production and the Oriental despot.

Isaac Deutscher in his Stalin biography says that one cannot situate the Stalin phenomenon as a mere Jacobian problem and in Robespierre's "reign of terror".[213] Despite the parallels—Stalin allied initially with the right-wing within the Bolsheviks (led by Bukharin) to exterminate the leftists (led by Trotsky) and then after destroying them, executed the rightists—Stalinism is a concrete phenomena and cannot be reduced to abstract analysis.

Liberal thinkers claim that Stalinism and violence are inbuilt in Marxism (especially Leninism) and that there is no restricting the party to represent *all* the people, thus not restricting the party to act as the dictatorship of the proletariat. According to this liberal thesis, the party is everything, and that in claiming to abolish the state, it is actually abolishing democracy. Owing to this illiberal "lack", Marxism could only be perpetually bound to anarchy and chaos. Deutscher talks of the "irrational urges inherent in despotism issued from revolution".[214] Bolshevism, according to Deutscher, "resisted the gods that were athirst".[215] But then how did Stalin create a system that demanded "absolute submission" as Khrushchev says, "to his opinion"?[216]

The view that something is inherently chaotic in Political Marxism, or the roots of Stalinism lay in Leninism is historically untenable. Consider Erich Fromm:

> The general habit of considering Stalinism and present-day Communism as identical with, or, at least a continuation

> of revolutionary Marxism has also led to an increasing misunderstanding of the personalities of great revolutionary figures: Marx, Engels, Lenin and Trotsky. Just as their theories are seen as related to those of Stalin and Khrushchev, the picture of the "revolutionary fanatic" is applied to them as it is applied to the vengeful killer Stalin, and to the opportunistic conservative Khrushchev. This distortion is a real loss for the present and the future. In whatever way one may disagree with Marx, Engels, Lenin and Trotsky, there can be no doubt that as persons they represent a flowering of Western humanity.[217]

So was there despotism in Lenin's party? Did Lenin throw out Zinoviev and Kamenev when they went to the Menshevik paper *Novaya Zhizn* on October 18, 1917 stating the date of the Bolshevik insurrection, thus almost sabotaging the revolution? The answer is simply no! Both continued as leaders of the revolution and close aides of Lenin.

So why the madness of Stalin? Why when he had already consolidated power and when the bureaucracy of the NEP-men as the managers of state capitalism in the Soviet Union was stabilized, did Stalin opt for mass murder? Why the mass killing of not only Lenin's close comrades, but workers, intellectuals, doctors and the public at large? And why in the late 1930s when the fascists had already the Soviet Union in their demonical sights?

The answer is that the bureaucracy needed for its own existence the elimination of the revolutionaries. What Trotsky called a "new ruling caste" developed where "the overwhelming majority of the older generation of the present bureaucracy had stood on the other side of the barricades during the October Revolution".[218] Trotsky talks of the "degeneration of the party".[219] Actually it was the transformation from a party of the revolution to the bureaucratic state. According to Joseph Hansen, the Moscow bureaucracy was a "privileged ruling caste"[220], this caste that was acting as the Overlords of the state capitalist restoration in the Soviet Union.

And here it must be noted that the Stalinist state was modelled after the Asiatic caste-clan system where a "slavish imitation" of caste and rank worship followed.[221] This New Caste-Class created a "new aristocracy".[222] This New Caste spoke in the name of the revolution. In actuality it was the gravedigger of this very revolution. The despot headed the counterrevolution from within. This New Caste was inherently unstable. Thus the continuous need for violence by this unstable New Caste. But below this New Caste stood classes that that had been terrified such that they seemed akin to the small-holding peasants that Marx had critiqued in *The Eighteenth Brumaire of Louis Bonaparte*:

> They are consequently incapable of enforcing their class interests in their own name, whether through a parliament or through a convention. They cannot represent themselves, they must be represented. Their representative must at the same time as their master, as an authority over them, as an unlimited governmental power that protects them against the other classes and sends them rain and sunshine from above.[223]

While Stalin appears as Timur, he also appears as Louis Bonaparte:

> But let there be no misunderstanding. The Bonaparte dynasty represents not the revolutionary, but the conservative peasant; not the peasant that strikes out beyond the condition of his social existence, the small holding, but rather the peasant who wants to consolidate this holding, not the country folk who, linked up with the towns, want to overthrow the old order through their own energies, but on the contrary those who, in stupefied seclusion within this old order, want to see themselves and their small holdings saved and favoured by the ghost of the empire. It represents not the enlightenment, but the superstition of the peasant; not his judgment, but his prejudice; not his future, but his past; not his modern Cévennes, but his modern Vendée.[224]

Thus:

> France, therefore, seems to have escaped the despotism of a class only to fall back beneath the despotism of the individual, and what is more, beneath the authority of an individual without authority. The struggle seems to be settled in such a way that all classes, equally impotent and equally mute, fall on their knees before the rifle butt.[225]

One only has to replace the word "France" and put the word "Soviet Union" and we get the following:

> Every common interest was straightway severed from society counterposed to it as a higher general interest, snatched from the activity of society's members.[226]

Marx's words, "all revolutions perfected this machine instead of smashing it"[227] were totally erased by Stalin The problem with Stalinism with its massive bureaucracy and military organization is located here. The questions that need to be posed are: Would there be a state in socialism, a transitory state, or a state of a "transitory regime"?[228] Is there a "workers' state" that "resort(s) to the customary norms of wage payment"?[229] Yet it must be noted that for Trotsky, the Soviet Union was never socialist, "but a preparatory regime transitional from capitalism to socialism".[230]

Consequently instead of the "first phase of communist society" and "higher phase of communist society",[231] we have the "lowest stage of communism" and the "highest stage". We see that what is a "phase" in Marx becomes a "stage" in Trotsky. Is this difference merely verbal, a difference that merely stems from translation? Or is there a deeper meaning to this?

But to say that there is no difference between Trotsky and Stalin and that Trotsky would have been involved in the unspeakable cruelties is factually incorrect. Trotsky is reinventing the possibilities of communism in a backward agrarian society. What Trotsky says is that this communism in a backward peasant society needs a state, yes, but a "dying state" (as he recalls Lenin's *State and Revolution*).[232] This "dying state" is different from the "cult of the bureaucratic state".[233] Trotsky, after Lenin, talked of "liquidating this parasite", namely "officialdom and the standing army".[234] For Trotsky, unlike Stalin's worship of the bureaucratic state:

> The proletariat will shatter the old bureaucratic machine and create its own apparatus out of employees and workers.[235]

Asiatic Mode of Production Does Not Mean Stagnancy

The problem is that the new state apparatus of employees and workers metamorphosized into the ugly bureaucratic Stalinist apparatus. Behind this metamorphosis stands the Stalinist counterrevolution and behind this stand the Asiatic mode of production and the Oriental despot who would head this political economy. One must thus emphasize: The caste question as an enclosed system also emerged in the analysis of the Stalinist state. One cannot restrict this idea only to one despotic system, but must see where else it can be extended. One also cannot restrict this idea as merely constituted in primitive division of labour.[236] Nor can we take the even more anti-Marxist view (the one that the once ideologue of the CPI(M) E.M.S. Namboodiripad had theorized), namely that caste was an "advancement" in the Indian mode of production.[237] Even worse is the idea propounded by Krishna Pillai one of the founders of the Communist Party in Kerala that "communism believes that the whole world belongs to one caste, i.e. the human caste."[238]

In contrast to the reductionist, teleological and romantic view of understanding caste, let us locate caste as an overdeterminate problematic, an overdetermination that is (to borrow a term from Louis Althusser) "complexly-structurally unevenly determined",[239] which rises to a form of complexity that combines the issues of economic activity combined with culture and politics that has within its belly the mechanisms of economic class (as *closed class*), race and neurosis-psychosis. This problematic of overdetermination I am linking to Marx's problematic of human alienation. I keep the terrain of radical humanism in critiquing both caste and class societies. This philosophical setting has to be understood in the Asiatic mode of production. Let us see how this appears in Marx's *Capital*:

> Manufacture, in fact, produces the skill of the detailed labourer by reproducing, and systematically driving to an extreme within the workshop, the naturally developed differentiation of trades which it found ready to hand in society at large. On the other hand, the conversion of fractional work into the life-calling of one man, corresponds to the tendency shown by earlier societies, to make trades hereditary; either to petrify them into castes, or whenever definite historical conditions beget in the individual a tendency to vary in a manner incompatible with the nature of castes, to ossify them into guilds. Castes and guilds arise from the action of the same natural law, that regulates the differentiation of plants and animals into species and varieties, except that, when a certain degree of development has been reached, the heredity of castes and the exclusiveness of guilds are ordained as a law of society.
>
> "The muslins of Dakka in fineness, the calicoes and other piece goods of Coromandel in brilliant and durable colours, have never been surpassed. Yet they are produced without capital,

machinery, division of labour, or any of those means which give such facilities to the manufacturing interest of Europe. The weaver is merely a detached individual, working a web when ordered by a customer, and with a loom of the rudest construction, consisting sometimes of a few branches or bars of wood, put roughly together. There is even no expedient for rolling up the warp; the loom must therefore be kept stretched to its full length, and becomes so inconveniently large, that it cannot be contained within the hut of the manufacturer, who is therefore compelled to ply his trade in the open air, where it is interrupted by every vicissitude of the weather." It is only the special skill accumulated from generation to generation, and transmitted from father to son, that gives to the Hindu, as it does to the spider, this proficiency. And yet the work of such a Hindu weaver is very complicated, compared with that of a manufacturing labourer.[240]

And a few pages later we have this:

Those small and extremely ancient Indian communities, some of which have continued down to this day, are based on possession in common of the land, on the blending of agriculture and handicrafts, and on an unalterable division of labour, which serves, whenever a new community is started, as a plan and scheme ready cut and dried. Occupying areas of from a hundred up to several thousand acres, each forms a compact whole producing all it requires. The chief part of the products is destined for direct use by the community itself, and does not take the form of a commodity. Hence, production here is independent of that division of labour brought about, in Indian society as a whole, by means of the exchange of commodities. It is the surplus alone that becomes a commodity, and a portion of even that, not until it has reached the hands of the State, into whose hands from time immemorial a certain quantity of these products has found its way in the shape of rent in kind. The constitution of these communities varies in different parts of India. In those of the simplest form, the land is tilled in common, and the produce divided among the members. At the same time, spinning and weaving are carried on in each family as subsidiary industries. Side by side with the masses thus occupied with one and the same work, we find the "chief inhabitant," who is judge, police, and tax-gatherer in one; the book-keeper, who keeps the accounts of the tillage

> and registers everything relating thereto; another official, who prosecutes criminals, protects strangers travelling through and escorts them to the next village; the boundary man, who guards the boundaries against neighbouring communities; the water-overseer, who distributes the water from the common tanks for irrigation; the Brahmin, who conducts the religious services; the schoolmaster, who on the sand teaches the children reading and writing; the calendar-Brahmin, or astrologer, who makes known the lucky or unlucky days for seed-time and harvest, and for every other kind of agricultural work; a smith and a carpenter, who make and repair all the agricultural implements; the potter, who makes all the pottery of the village; the barber, the washerman, who washes clothes, the silversmith, here and there the poet, who in some communities replaces the silversmith, in others the schoolmaster. This dozen of individuals is maintained at the expense of the whole community. If the population increases, a new community is founded, on the pattern of the old one, on unoccupied land. The whole mechanism discloses a systematic division of labour; but a division like that in manufactures is impossible, since the smith and the carpenter, &c., find an unchanging market, and at the most there occur, according to the sizes of the villages, two or three of each, instead of one. The law that regulates the division of labour in the community acts with the irresistible authority of a law of Nature, at the same time that each individual artificer, the smith, the carpenter, and so on, conducts in his workshop all the operations of his handicraft in the traditional way, but independently, and without recognizing any authority over him. The simplicity of the organization for production in these self-sufficing communities that constantly reproduce themselves in the same form, and when accidentally destroyed, spring up again on the spot and with the same name—this simplicity supplies the key to the secret of the unchangeableness of Asiatic societies, an unchangeableness in such striking contrast with the constant dissolution and refounding of Asiatic States, and the never-ceasing changes of dynasty. The structure of the economic elements of society remains untouched by the storm-clouds of the political sky.[241]

As I noted before, the idea of the Asiatic mode of production that Marx had highlighted is not to be understood as a Eurocentric reading of India and Asia. It is not the case that Asia suffered from civilizational sluggishness that could only be overcome with the interaction with European civilization and capitalism. Instead one is talking of this mode of production in concrete empirical terms. Recall that in the early 1770s the GDP of India was 27 per cent of the world's GDP, in 1800 it went down to 23 per cent and then in 1947 it was reduced to 3 per cent. It is colonialism that drained the wealth and which broke the unity of manufacture and agriculture and thus which broke the backbone of Indian pre-colonial Indian economy. It was also colonialism that made India literally "illiterate". In 1947 only 17 per cent of India was literate. Thus when we say that caste—in the Indic variation of this mode—is central to this mode of production, we need to exactly define by what one means by "caste". "Caste" should not confused with "community". What will be recognized is that we have a dialectic of caste and community in the operation of the pre-colonial mode. How "labouring communities" are transfigured as "castes" (or "enclosed and hierarchical classes") remains to be seen.

That is why it is important to note, as I had said in *Why We Are Not Hindus* and also in my *In the Name of Marx* that Edward Said was totally wrong in thinking that the "legacy" of the Asiatic mode of production is rooted in the thirteenth century translation of Aristotle's *Politics* and consequently with the development of a "science" of politics by Machiavelli. The messenger boy from Asia to Marx was not Francois Bernier. Neither was Bernier's *Travels in the Mogul Empire, 1656-68* nor his *A New Division of the Earth* where the world was said to be divided into different "races", the texts of Marx's scientific reference. Instead for Marx, it was the manner that surplus was extracted (as "tax-rent"), the caste-clan division of society, the principle that there was no property in land and the sovereign as the "Oriental despot" that formed the contours of his understanding of the Asiatic mode of production. That is why I insist that Marx's ideas of the Asiatic mode along with his idea of the Oriental Despot is not to be confused with either the Latin interpretations of Aristotle, Jean Bodin, Machiavelli, Montesquieu, Bayle, Bacon, Hobbes, Harrington and Francois Bernier, nor with Karl Wittfogel's *Oriental Despotism*. For Marx, the Asiatic mode of production is not a normative discourse created by travellers from Europe. For him, despotism means the "enclosed state".[242] And this analysis of enclosure was empirical, not normative. But this "enclosure" was not restricted to Asia. Marx writes that "Adam

Smith found evidences of enclosed life in Europe; he attacked in particular the close corporations and guilds...."[243]

One should be clear: the idea of the Asiatic mode of production is not a "civilizational" discourse that emerged in the cranium of the Orientalists. In this respect, consider Marx who says that "the close corporations of merchants and craftsmen in Europe had their history, as the products of a prior era when the preponderant wealth and power lay in the hands of the landed barons and gentry."[244] So when Marx talks of "close corporations" these are not restricted merely to Asia. That is why we are saying that the Asiatic mode of production is not a part of the awful "clash of civilizations" genre. Instead Marx's idea of the Asiatic mode of production is a specific concrete mode of production that could not be reduced to the same mechanisms of slave, feudal and capitalist societies of Western Europe. Marx, for instance, talks of the "growing differences between the two modes of production" (i.e. the Asiatic and European modes).[245] But one should not "overemphasize the difference from the European cities".[246] Asia, for Marx, was not the backyard of underdevelopment. The Asiatic mode of production does not imply that there was what Perry Anderson calls a "received opposition between Asia and Europe".[247] Thus:

> In the East, there were at first comparable developments. Science had been developed by the Mughal emperor, Ulug Bek, in the fifteenth-sixteenth centuries; Shah Abbas the Great, emperor of Persia, had fostered the industrial arts in his capital at Isfahan in the seventh century by importing skilled workers in textiles and metals, leather, wood and ceramics from neighbouring places in India and the Near East; these developments compared to the development of the sciences, industrial technology and arts in England, the Low Countries, Germany, France and Italy in the same periods.[248]

And because I am saying that one cannot reduce the histories of Asia to Europe, I am also saying that Irfan Habib's talking of "potentialities of capitalist development in the economy of Mughal India"[249] is wrong since the argument is based on the reductionist idea of self-evolving forces of production narrative. Habib almost conveniently forgets the argument of primitive accumulation of capital that forms the basis for capitalism to emerge. He instead (as a master teleologist) talks of not merely "potentialities of growth", but "potentialities of capitalist development" and the "possible road to modern industry" as sole markers of capitalism.[250] We know that Marx argued often that Western capitalism cannot be used as a signifier of universalism. Take his 1877 letter to the Narodniki journal where he warns that there is a difference between concrete analysis of concrete conditions and applying metaphysical methodologies.[251]

Yet it is also necessary to state the researches of Kevin Anderson who pointed out to an epistemic break in Marx's works on Asia, where he says that 1858 turned out to be a "turning point".[252] Consequently instead of merely seeing Marx's articles for the *New York Tribune* as his alleged "articles on India", it is better to understand the repertoire of pre-capitalist societies that he articulated in the *Grundrisse* which finally culminated in his *Ethnological Notebooks.*

What contemporary capitalism has done in India is what Marx says in *Capital* Vol. III, namely that the expansion of production was more or less impossible such that it reduced the direct producers to the physical minimum of means of subsistence.[253] And because the Asiatic state is a highly centralized state, where "the power of the sovereign was absolute, had no rivals, eliminated all rivals"[254], where the state as the "supreme lord"[255] rules the roost, anti-state politics of the people "from below" has to be the bulwark of the Indian revolution. The subaltern castes who serve as the pool of surplus labour and parts of the surplus population would now become essential parts of the revolution. They can in no way be called "lumpen". A revolution is necessary, a revolution against both the Caste Overlord and capitalism, a revolution that did not have to go through the bourgeois stage of development. It was both Marx and Ambedkar who had seen this alternative. For both (Marx and Ambedkar) non-Western societies had to go for a "direct communism".

The Asiatic mode thus gets a new and fresh setting. That is why I say that this Asiatic mode of production is a concrete mode of production—or better a set of concrete modes of production—where in India caste plays a pivotal role such that one can also describe India as having a caste mode of production. This mode of production has its own internal historical and social mechanisms. As we shall see there will be three different structures in this mode: (1) the centralized state, (2) village communities, or modes of production determined by caste-clans and labouring communities, and (3) classless communes. Marx thought that the third existed in Russia in the 1880s and these communes could *directly* lead the socialist revolution:

> If the Russian Revolution becomes the signal for proletarian revolution in the West, so that the two complement each other, then present Russia's peasant communal land-ownership may serve as the starting point for a communist development.[256]

This point one has to understand. The implication is that the politics of the annihilation of caste could directly lead to communism and that capitalism need not intervene in Asian histories. What I am doing thus is challenging the unilinear theory of history that Stalin had sanctified and which the Indian Left by and large never challenged. What this unilinear theory propagated was that history is determined by so-called "iron laws" and that each stage of history was "inevitable". The fact that this thesis was only a disguised and secularized form of messianic theology was never considered by the Indian Left. And also that this messianic theology left out a large part of the world should also be pointed out.

In contrast to these messianic versions of socialism, one has to note that this "direct communism" would have to necessarily usher in an International in Asia where the flames of the revolution would also topple not only the Caste Overlords in India, but also the Pakistani generals and the Iranian Ayatollahs. One will have to note that as "civilized peoples", one necessarily has to be in "close relation with one another". [257]

One has to insist alongside Engels (and against the Indian Left) that the "communist revolution, therefore, will be not merely a national one; it will take place in all civilized countries..." [258] One cannot like the nineteenth century revolutionaries imagine that one can "consummate a proletariat revolution within the national walls of France".[259]

These remarks are pertinent to contemporary India. Just as Marx is against French endogamy, we must point out that an Indian form of endogamy and an Indian form of "revolution in one country" will be impossible. But the first move for this form of Asian internationalism, is the programme of the annihilation of caste. Since caste signifies "small semi-barbarian, semi-civilized communities",[260] a necessary transcendence of this barbaric state is necessary. One has to note that Marx (contra Irfan Habib and Edward Said) contrasts the "small semi-barbarian, semi-civilized communities" with the "inherent barbarism of bourgeois civilization".[261] Marx is in no way an Orientalist. The difference between Asian history and West European one is not guided by (to recall Said) "an imaginary line drawn somewhere between Greece and Turkey (which) was called the Orient".[262] The question is of concrete historicization.

Kevin Anderson, for instance, says that there is a "radical difference between Asian and West European economic history."[263] For instance, usury in pre-capitalist India did not lead to the revolutionizing of relations of production. Instead it "persisted for a long time without leading to anything more than economic decay and political corruption".[264] What Marx in his economic manuscripts talks of is the dominance of usury and the suppression of the capitalist mode of production. This pertains more than not to India. Consider Marx:

> Thus even the *formal capital-relation* does not take place, still less the specifically capitalist mode of production....It is rather a form which *makes labour sterile*, places it under the most unfavourable economic conditions, and combines together *capitalist exploitation without a capitalist mode of production* (last two emphasis mine, M.J.), and the mode of independent small-scale property in the instruments of labour without the advantages this mode of production offers for less developed conditions. Here the means of production have ceased to belong to the producer, but they are *nominally* subsumed to him; and the means of production remain in the same relations of small independent enterprise, only the relations are in ruins.[265]

Note this idea of "ruins" with the idea of *Untergangs* that Marx mentions in his 1873 Afterword to the Second German Edition of *Capital*, Vol. I[266] and the idea of the "world of woes" from his 'The British Rule in India'.[267] I relate these ideas with Anderson mentioning Marx's statement that the Indian peasant "merely vegetates in the most miserable manner."[268] What is important is that there is (to recall Anderson once again) a "radical difference" between Asian and West European histories after the dissolution of the primitive gens.

Here it is important to point out that caste is not an inherent civilizational problem of India. It would not require capitalism and parliamentary democracy, inspired by bourgeois Europe and USA, to rescue India from the spectre of caste. Instead it would be (to borrow Marx's famous expression) a "fundamental revolution in the social state of Asia"[269] that would rescue India from the caste system. We know that middle class Dalit politicians lead to the utter bourgeoisification of the Dalit movement. There is no evidence that post-Ambedkar there have ever been Dalit politicians who have challenged this system. None want to talk of capitalism and imperialism. Almost all of them could be said to be the worshipers of capitalism and imperialism. We also know that these worshippers of capitalism and imperialism have deified Macaulay and have utter contempt for revolutionary politics. These Stalinists of the Dalit movement imagine that capitalism would emancipate Dalits. What this form of politics does is that it mimes the colonial narrative of the "civilization mission of capitalism and imperialism". That is why many Dalit thinkers imagine that it is Western imperialism that will emancipate them. Some also write odes to Macaulay. Middle class Dalit politics becomes utterly bourgeois through and through, especially in their fear of the "class question". They fear this class question, they fear the word "class", because of their fear of being proletarianized. But what they probably do not understand, that it is the same fear which forms the essence of fascist politics. In contrast to this form of Dalit politics of talism and also in contrast to the Orientalist imperialist cartography that produced a great abyss between the "rational West" from an imagined "irrational East" thereby deducing a form of *absolute peculiarity* of the East, one needs to understand what one calls the mode of "relative peculiarity",[270] contextualized in a form of concreteness of social phenomena. Thus in contrast to the thesis of a great abyss of the West from the East, I shall talk of what is known since Trotsky as *combined and uneven development*.

For the proletariat of the West to be emancipated, not only is a proletariat revolution in their respective countries necessary, but along with this is the necessity of revolution in the whole of Asia and Africa. Likewise for a revolution in Asia and Africa—a revolution against caste-clan capitalism headed by the Caste Overlords and the financial oligarchs—an international revolution is necessary.

And since the struggle is internationalist, the simple national struggles within nations will have to be transcended (*aufgohoben*) for larger struggles. National struggles from within respective nation states will give no results. For example, struggles within the nation states of India, Pakistan, Nepal, Sri Lanka, Bangladesh, etc. would be meaningless if not coordinated with struggles of the Asian Soviets. A radical reimagining of revolution will thus have to be done.

The Indian Left, the Liberals and the Asiatic Mode of Production

Except for Shireen Moosvi[271], no Indian historian has seriously analyzed Marx's original idea of the Asiatic mode of production. A small note on this writing of history by the Indian Left which has totally forgotten Marx's original contribution is thus necessary. Irfan Habib in his seminal essay 'Marx's Perception of India' refutes this very important idea. He does not even vaguely refer to Marx's *Ethnological Notebooks* which was published in the mid-1970s. Why is this the case? Why does Habib stubbornly refuse to read Marx's very important text? [272] Why does he only mention the 1959 and 1976 Moscow editions of Marx on India, alongside selected correspondence between Marx and Engels [273] as if these are enough to bring a clear Marxist view of India? Since Habib (and one should say all those who subscribe to the erroneous theory of "Indian feudalism") does not take the extreme complex dialectic of the communes, village communities and the authoritarian Asiatic state as a dialectic of combined and uneven social formations, he reduces Marx to an Orientalist-like thinker.[274] But why does Habib refer to Marx as a fellow traveller of not only Hegel, but also Macaulay?[275] Can this great doyen of Marxist history be called "revolutionary"? Further why does he say that Marx had a "mystical view of property"[276] and he also worked with "inherited generalizations"?[277] Is then Habib the great Left historian actually a revisionist?

The problem is constituted deeply in a theoretical framework, the framework that could not overthrow the upper caste (read Brahmanical biases). Note R.S. Sharma talking of the Kali Age.[278] He refers to elite literature and history "from above". Unlike Sharad Patil and Gail Omvedt he nowhere refers to subaltern bahujan literature. He does not talk of the Kali Age as the dystopia of the Caste Overlords. His reference point is itself the point of the elites.

What I would like to state that unlike R.S. Sharma and the Indian Left historians and even unlike Sharad Patil and Gail Omvedt, it is necessary to go into Marx's original repertoire. Here Anderson's *Marx at the Margins* serves us best. One also has to go through Marx's *Grundrisse* seriously along with Marx's 1861-65 Economic Manuscripts. What I will say is that Habib makes sweeping statements about Marx (on the Asiatic mode). Anderson never does that. It is important to analyze each of Marx's texts in their respective contexts. Take Marx in his 1861-63 Manuscripts where he talks of the "Asiatic forms of land ownership still in existence".[279] Consequently:

> The natural laws of the ancient, the Asiatic, or the feudal mode of production were essentially different.[280]

Now it is well known that Indian Marxism, by and large, shares an ambivalent relation to the caste question because Marx's views on the non-capitalist, non-Western world were ignored whereby the history of Western Europe (especially the question of the transition of feudalism to capitalism in Europe) was imposed as a readymade model to be imposed on *all* societies. This fallacy has been disastrous for not only the Indian revolution, but also for Indian democracy, as the subject of both revolution and democracy could not be found. To talk of the industrial proletariat as the revolutionary subject independent of the concrete history of South Asia (as theorized by the mainstream Parliamentary Left), or to talk of the peasants as the subject of Indian history (as the Indian Maoists do), are abstract questions posed, questions which are independent of the real history of South Asia, thus independent of the history of social structures that comprise castes (and if not pre-capitalist communities then at least non-capitalist communities) would turn out to be a form of social engineering that is totally alien to the spirit of science.

One has thus to be careful about terminology. That is why it is important once more to put a small note on Marx's characterization of the Oriental despot. Marx's idea of this Oriental despot is not in any way opposed to the alleged "free thinking liberal European". The "despot" is not an Aurangzeb or a Bahdur Shah Zafar. One has to note this as the following:

> For the British after 1857, the Indian Muslim became an almost subhuman creature, to be classified in an unembarrassingly racist imperialist literature alongside such other despised and subject specimens such as Irish Catholics or 'the Wandering Jew'. The depth to which Indian Muslims had sunk in British eyes is visible in an 1868 production called *The People of India*, which contains photographs of the different castes and tribes of South Asia.....[281]

For Marx, the critique is a critique of the Indian elites, a critique that has to be situated in the critique of the caste mode of production and the cultural politics of the elites:

> Now, sickening as it must be to human feeling to witness those myriads of industrious patriarchal and inoffensive social organizations disorganized and dissolved into their units, thrown into a sea of woes, and their individual members losing at the same time their ancient form of civilization, and their hereditary means of subsistence, we must not forget that idyllic village communities, inoffensive though they may appear, (which) had always been the solid foundation of Oriental Despotism, that they had restrained the human mind within the smallest compass, making it the unresisting tool of superstition, enslaving it beneath traditional rules, depriving it of all grandeur and historical energies. We must not forget that the barbarian egotism which, concentrating on some miserable piece of land, had quietly witnessed the ruin of empires, the perpetuation of unspeakable cruelties, the massacre of the population of large towns, with no other consideration bestowed upon them than on natural events, itself the helpless prey of any aggressor who designed to notice it at all. We must not forget that this undignified, stagnatory, and vegetative life, that this passive sort of existence evoked on the one part, in contradistinction, wild, aimless, unbounded forces of destruction and rendered murder itself a religious rite in Hindustan. We must not forget that these little communities were contaminated by caste and slavery, that they subjugated man to external circumstances, that they transformed a self-developing social state into never changing natural destiny, and thus brought about a brutalizing worship of nature, exhibiting its degradation in the fact that man, the sovereign of nature, fell down on his knees in adoration of Hanuman the monkey, and Sabbala, the cow. England, it is true, in causing a

social revolution in Hindostan, was actuated only by the vilest interests, and was stupid in her manner of enforcing them. But that is not the question. The question is, can mankind fulfill its destiny without a fundamental revolution in the social state of Asia? If not, whatever may have been the crimes of England she was the unconscious tool of history in bringing about that revolution. Then, whatever bitterness the spectacle of the crumbling of an ancient world may have for our personal feelings, we have the right, in point of history, to exclaim with Goethe:

Sollte these Qual uns quälen
Da sie unsre Lust vermehrt,
Hat nicht myriaden Seelen
Timur's Herrschaft aufgezehrt?

"Should this torture then torment us
Since it brings us greater pleasure?
Were not through the rule of Timur
Souls devoured without measure?" [282]

For Marx, the rule of caste and the Oriental despot (whether Timur or Manu) gave way for souls that were devoured without measure. That is why it needs to be pointed out that Marx was no Orientalist who was debunking Timur. Instead what I am saying is that the above stated passage is not an "offensive" passage. Instead what I would like to note is the parallel between Marx and Ambedkar's critique of caste that can be derived from the above quote from Marx. Marx's passages, one must insist, correspond to those of Phule and Ambedkar.[283] Note the idea of the "restraining the human mind within the smallest compass" which equals the critique of "the idiocy of rural life" in feudal Europe.[284] What I would also like to note is that this idea of caste as restraining of the human mind can also be linked to Marx's idea of the estranged mind that he outlines in his *Economic and Philosophic Manuscripts of 1844*.

Caste is necessarily meant to suppress and enslave humanity.[285] It is this iron cage of caste which we now need to relate with the idea of the *closed society*. When Marx is talking of the sluggishness and the stagnancy in Indian society it is because of this realm of "closure". What the Oriental despot did was that he did not put the surplus into circulation, but either consumed it—thus got involved in unproductive consumption—or had the same devoured by the unnecessary ritualism of the priestly caste who with their infamous practice of Yagna destroyed the surplus. And in this "Great Sacrifice" not only were animals butchered to please both the gods as well as the priests, but also humanity was stunted because of the totem of purity and the taboo of pollution and the consequent practice of untouchability. My emphasis is on the linking of caste with the generic idea of the Asiatic mode of production and that of the infamous Orientalist despot who devours human souls. Gogol's classic *Dead Souls* may also come in to give life to this discussion of the caste system as a totalitarian and closed system that speaks the language of what Theodor Adorno calls the "administered world", the world of "the solid foundation of Oriental despotism"[286] which celebrates the "wild aimless, unbounded forces of destruction",[287] which is based on "a sort of equilibrium, resulting from a general repulsion and constitutional exclusiveness, resulting between all its members".[288] Not only is caste the foundation of what I insist on calling "Oriental despotism", it is also the solid foundation of the "inherited evils"[289] that yet possess and haunt modern India. Caste has not left us. Gandhi tried to romanticize caste and this was his terrible counterrevolutionary role in Indian history. Nehru tried to sweep caste under the carpet imagining that modern industries (to be precise dams) as the "temples of modern India" would dissolve caste.

That is why it is pertinent to say that in contrast to the liberal's forgetfulness of caste (Gandhi and Nehru are only two examples), as well as in contrast to the Established Left that has made a fetish of class (here one means that only modern economic class matters—in fact a European idea of class—and nothing else) and thus ignored the dialectic of caste and class, one needs keeping this dialectic central in order to understand how actual class formations and modern bourgeois state power enter the scene of Indian history.

One also needs to tell the Established Indian Left, who seem not to have read Marx critically, that by "modes of production" Marx means something much more profound than what the economist inspired Left imagines it to be so. Consider Marx:

> Religion, family, state, law, morality, science, art, etc., are only *particular* modes of production, and fall under its general law (i.e. the law of estrangement, private property and the production of reified consciousness. My insertion: M. J.).[290]

One also needs to inform this same "Marx-less leftist" that Lenin had based his revolutionary politics on the radical critique of economism. Taking this into consideration, as also taking into consideration that caste like religion, family, state, law and morality are all modes of production, we insert caste as not only some aberration of Indian society, but as a very well defined social structure, so deep-rooted that we call after Hegel as the essence or the *Wesen* of India's social being. Caste, as Marx said, "makes labour sterile".[291] In this sense India with its essence of caste is nothing but the personification of sterility. And on this sterile foundation, the Indian Caste Overlords built their entire apparatus, especially their apparatus of economic dependency, cultural castration, transcendental theology and political domination.

Thus what I say is that if Nehru thought that industries and dams are the temples of modern India, little would he know that in today's "post-truth" world, *temples would become the industries and dams of postmodern, post-truthful India.* Temples, and the discourses of temples since the early 1990s after the savage destruction of the Babri mosque at Ayodhya, would be the return of the repressed.

Caste as the Return of the Repressed

Our "post-honest" politician would say that caste has never existed. And when the brute nature would be pointed out this "post-honest" politician would say that it was probably Islam that brought caste to India. Some would even say that caste is something good for India and only when the caste mode of production is prevalent that the Indian economy flourishes and that the GDP is high only where caste economies operate. To dispel these right-wing myths, one must understand what caste means. Remember that the Indian terms are "*varna*" and "*jati*" and these form an essential part of the Indian lexicography. Despite these terms, I will say that the modern term "*caste*" is precise to define its characteristic, as it signifies a type of *closed and fragmented society*.

It is well known that though the word "caste" is itself derived from the Latin *castus* meaning "pure, segregated, cut off", it is etymologically related to *carere* "to cut off" and sociologically related to the formation of hierarchical clan groups. The cutting is evident since the foundational myth in the *Rg Veda*.[292] Thus if any nationalist votary of caste claims that the word "caste" itself is embedded in Latinized discourse, this would be entirely wrong. What is important to understand is that because caste implies the logic of "cutting off", it gets to be directly related to alienation. And that is why I point out the relation between alienation as *Entfremdung* that arouses the feeling of loneliness and helplessness that Marx highlights in his *Economic and Philosophic Manuscripts of 1844* with the caste system. But I do not merely relate these two. I also relate caste as alienation to Freud's concept of *Unheimlich* or the "uncanny" that raises the feeling of dread and terror.[293] Caste creates dread and horror. One has to transcend this terrible system.

It is after this new epistemic location that one needs to study the historical materialist study of caste. I have said in my *The New Militants* that social science has attempted to locate a manifold origin of caste: from the Indo-Iranian origins to the period from the rise of Buddhism to the Gupta period.[294] What is important that the historical materialist genealogy and structural analysis of caste is necessary. While the scientific point of view locates caste in the complex of social formations that is itself based on a form of labour process that produces surplus,[295] it is necessary to understand the breakdown of the old commune systems (*Ganas* in India). Removing caste from this space of the breakdown of the *Gana* system would only make the reading of the caste question extremely unscientific.

When I have said that caste has to be seen as the dialectical essence (*Wesen*) of Indian history, it does not have to be understood as an essentialist argument the way Louis Dumont argued in *Homo Hierarchicus*. The unfortunate, neurotic and tragic part is that caste as dialectical essence could modify and manipulate every ideology and political movement that came in its way. Forget Buddhism, Christianity and Islam. Even modernity did not allow the uprooting of this system. This is where I apply *Freud's theory of neurosis as the eternal recurrence of the same trauma with the persistence of caste*. For what happened is that despite Buddhism's anti-Vedic worldview and despite Islam's egalitarianism, the Buddhist and Muslim rulers not only did not challenge caste, but used it for their own advantage. Albêrûnî's writings are an example of an Iranian-Muslim anthropologist's (almost) celebration of caste. (We shall look at the details below.) The persistence of caste throughout the ages has to be mentioned, including the times of Buddhism and Islam. So why was caste present despite Buddhism and Islam?[296] Though Habib raises this paradox: persistence of caste even in the times of Buddhism and Islam, he however does not link caste with the Asiatic mode. Habib does not bother to explain this fact. Why is caste persistent in India? Habib almost stubbornly refuses to engage the Asiatic mode of production. It is the terrain of taboo which he would not ever enter, a taboo that would haunt political Marxism in India.

What I am saying is that because of the Indic variation of the Asiatic mode of production that despite anti-caste religious ideologies, in Buddhist and Islamic times, caste still persists. What is important is to see the material reality—the geographical part in historical materialism—and thus see that caste is not merely an idealist conspiracy of the Brahman elites independent of the questions of economic structure of society, but is instead seen as being located in particular social formations, that despite the death of these social formations, it yet exists in brutal and savage form. And that is why I say that the idea of "neurosis-psychosis" has to be brought into the understanding of the persistence of caste.

A concrete scientific analysis of caste has to be located. One could ask: Is caste only a feature of India, and only because of the dominance of Brahmanical ideology, does it persist? Or would Pakistan, Afghanistan and Iran also have caste like social formations? Or should one say that there are "clan" formations in those parts of the world and not caste? Why did Trotsky use the term "caste" when describing the counterrevolutionary bureaucracy under Stalin? Further how does one understand how in almost similar social formations, existing in India and Iran in medieval times, in one case (India) caste was prominently present, and in the other (Iran) it did not prevail?[297] Or can we say that a different type of closed society existed in medieval Iran determined by the clan system? Or would we say that the Iranian version of the Asiatic mode of production gives way to different results, which do not correspond to the Indian variant?

It must be said that despite at least one hundred years of serious research the origins of caste remains a perplexing question. We know of the theories of Georges Dumezil, D.D. Kosambi, Irfan Habib and Gherardo Gnoli. What I intend to do is to bring in the Avestean narrative in the understanding of caste and the hegemony of the caste-elites. In this historical analysis one traces the domination of these Indo-Iranian military elites. I am locating the hegemony of caste within the narrative of the Indo-Iranian military elite. The four castes can be divided into two Great Classes:

1. The warrior-priests, and
2. The producing communities.

The first group is essentially a parasitic clan that literally lives on the destruction of the surplus. Yagna, or the Great Vedic Sacrifice is an example of this destruction of the economic surplus. Buddhism and Jainism consequently emerged as the ideological critique (as protest) of the destruction of the surplus and the violence of the warrior-priests. Indra in the *Rg Veda* stands for the archetypal warrior-priest, the Indian warrior-gladiator *Kshatriya* and the Iranian *Rathaēštars. Rathaēštars* are literally "the wielders of the chariot" in Persian. The period of this great class struggle is located in the Late Bronze Age. One thus has to locate the date of the discovery of bronze and the consequent production of the chariot as the vehicle for raiding pastoral communities in order to understand the birth of the military elites in Indo-Iranian history. According to this narrative, mastered by Gnoli, the primary class struggle was between these warrior tribes (the Indian *Kshatriyas* and the Iranian *Rathaēštars*) and the agriculturalists (the Indian *Vaiśyas* and the Iranian *Vastryō.fšuyants*).[298]

However in the beginning whether *originally* there were three or four caste groups is not sufficiently known. True the 10th mandala in the *Rg Veda* talks of four caste-groups. Sometimes it is theorized that originally there were three caste groups.[299] It was Georges Dumezil (1898-1986) who in 1929 talked of the trifunctional ideology where proto-Indo-European society was said to be divided into three classes: the priests, warriors and the working multitude (the farmers, herders, craftspeople and traders) which corresponded to the three great economic activities: the sacred, political and economic production. Thus sovereignty, military and productivity were the three basic activities that Dumezil said were basic to Indo-European society. It is not exactly clear as to how and why in the Indian subcontinent that these three classes got reified into castes with its corresponding theological sanction, while also producing the "Great Refusal" in the form of the Śūdra and the outcaste and untouchable ati-Śūdra communities. Thus the perplexing questions are: From whence came the fourth caste? And consequently from whence from outside this four caste system (*Chaturvarnaya*) did the ati-Śūdra caste emerge?

The spectre of fascism is always around when discussing caste and ancient Indian society. While anthropology gives credence to Dumezil for inventing the tripartite division of society in the three great classes, well before him Arthur de Gobineau (1816-1882) talked of this, but with clear-cut racist implications. In his *An Essay on the Inequality of the Human Races* he mentioned how aristocrats were from the "Aryan" stock and thus superior to the plebian masses. How racist ideology in the aftermath of the 1848 revolutions in Europe developed this racist theory to counter the nascent proletarian socialist movement has to be noted. One must state how rigorous science is distinct from ideology.

One must thus note however that in this original tripartite division of society (of Dumezil) in the three great classes, there is a shared code between the Indians, Iranians, Romans, Greeks and Germans. One must note the genetic affinity between the upper castes in South Asia with Europeans, while the lower castes are more like Asians has to be pointed out. A 2001 study of Michale Bamshad of the Eccles Institute of Human Genetics of the University of Utah in the journal *Genome Research*[300] pointing to these conclusions also verifies Phule's thesis of the upper caste elites being parts of the invading Indo-European stock. In this sense the idea that caste-stratification was according to the principle of race and colour ("*varna*") is correct.

To go to classical references, one needs to go to the study of Indo-Iranian societies and thus need to go to Albêrûnî who points to this apparent "race-based" classification regarding the Indian castes. In his chapter 'On the Castes, called "Colours" (Varna), and on the Classes below them', in his magnum opus *India* Albêrûnî talks of the phantasmagorical "genius" of the ancient Indo-Iranian kings who invented the caste system to prevent the "disorder" of intermixture.[301] Iran is also on the horizons of his thinking. For Albêrûnî, India is not alone in having this caste system. That there are echoes with the *Gita* which also forbids castes to mix has to be pointed out. But would the taboo of intermixture be a larger pre-capitalist phenomenon that would be part of many other social formations and cultures, besides India?

If Manu is seen as the diabolic lawmaker regarding caste and if Krishna in the *Gita* philosophizes on caste, in Iran it is the Faustian figure of Jamshid who is said to be the inventor of this terrible system. But then is this true? Why did this Iranian Faust invent caste? It must be noted that this legendary figure is the same one who appears earlier as Yima (in Old Persian) and Yama (in Old Sanskrit). Direct reference is found in the legendary long poem, the *Shâhnâma*, where Jamshid is said to have created the three *Anjuman* (literally "institutions" or "assemblies"). But then one must note that the Persian words are *Anjuman* and *Guroh* implying "assembly", "congregation", "troop" and "band" and not "caste".

The two sister civilizations—India and Iran—have a common grounding with different routes. But in the *Rg Veda* and *The Gathtas* (the original philosophical poem of Iran's prophet Zarathushtra) this Faustian figure is both a hero and a criminal[302]. He is, as Shaul Shaked says, "tainted by sin".[303] It must also be noted that there is a share code between the Indian and the Iranian narratives, but also with the Afghan one. Remember that in Afghanistan (even today) it is the same Yama who appears as the father of the Afghan people. Jamshid (in Iranian legend) not only creates classes. He also creates endogamy, the consanguine family, teaches warfare and weaving. Note that this consanguine family system is the essence of Hinduism and the caste system. The irony is that this legendary Indo-Iranian hero appears as both hero and sinner. This sin or crime is not mentioned. It seems that, if one brings in Marx, that he becomes a criminal in creating classes. For Freud, his crime is that he institutionalizes incest. In the *Rg Veda* he also appears as a fallen hero but for exactly opposite reasons, for he refuses to have sex with his sister Yami.[304] He then does not create endogamy, or if he does, is also responsible for breaking it. In the later part of the Zoroastrian magnum opus the *Avesta*, this crime-sin becomes clear. Jamshid is an atheist and refuses to accept the covenant that Ahura Mazda (the Persian rendering of God) offers him. Consider the dialogue between Ahura Mazda and Jamshid:

> Ahura Mazda: Do-you-accept of-me, fair Jam
> Son-of-Vivanghan the instruction and spread of religion?
>
> Jamshid: Neither am-I the giver nor teacher
> Of the instruction of the spread of-religion,-that-is, I cannot perform the work of teacher and disciple.[305]

In the above verse he is certainly a heroic figure. He "symbolizes divine power and presence in the world".[306] During his reign humanity does not know death. In the following verse from the Persian *Sháhnáma* this is how Yama/Yima as Jamshid appears. Once again this is a heroic rendering:

> Jamshid, the mighty son of Tahmuras,
> Full of his father's maxims, girt himself,
> Succeeded to his glorious father's throne,
> And wore in kingly wise the crown of gold.
> His girdle was the Grace of king of kings,
> And all the world obeyed him, contests ceased,
> The age had rest, and bird and div and fairy
> Were his to bid, the world took added lustre,
> Through him the throne of Shahs was glorified.
> "Mine is the Grace," he said, "I am both king
> And archimage, I will restrain ill-doers
> And make for souls a path towards the light."
> He first wrought arms and oped for warriors
> The door of fame. His Grace made iron yield;
> He fashioned it to helmets, hauberks, breastplates,
> And coats of armour both for man and horse.
> His ardent mind achieved the work and made
> Good store in fifty years. Another fifty
> He spent on raiment fit for fight or feast;
> And made of spun and floss silk, hair and cotton,
> Fine fabrics, cloth of hair and rich brocade.
> He taught to spin and weave, and when the stuffs

Were made he showed men how to full and sew them
Then to the joy of all he founded castes
For every craft; it took him fifty years,
Distinguishing one caste as sacerdotal
To be employed in sacred offices,
He separated it from other folk
And made its place of service on the mountains
That God might be adorned in quietude.
Arrayed for battle on the other hand
Were those who formed the military caste;
They were the lion-men inured to war—
The lights of armies and of the provinces—
Whose office was the guard the royal throne
And vindicate the nation's name for valour.
The third caste was the agricultural,
All independent tillers of the soil,
The sowers and the reapers—men whom none
Upbraideth when they eat. Though clothed in rags,
The weavers are not slaves, and sounds of chiding
Reach not their years. They are freemen and labour
Upon the safe soil from dispute and contest.
What said the noble man and eloquent?
"'Tis idleness that maketh freemen slaves".
The fourth caste was the artizens. They live
By doing handicraft—a turbulent crew
Who being always busied with their craft
Are given much to thought.[307]

It is in the later part of the *Avesta* that the Iranian "Fall" is mentioned. There is thus a "tragic ring" to the Jamshid narrative.[308] This "Fall" is because of Jamshid's radical refusal in accepting god.[309] And with this "fall" comes mortality. Humanity's greatest fear death is born. But does caste also originate with the "Fall"? In the *Rg Veda* the birth of the caste system emerges from the slaughter of primeval man. Caste is both the result of this Rg Vedic "Fall", as also that which is the balancing force to counter this "Fall". The *Rg Veda* also talks of "incest, kidnapping, procuring abortion as well as deceit, theft and robbery".[310] Yet it is only in one place in the *Rg Veda* that caste is mentioned, as we all very well know, it is of later dating. Likewise with caste, patriarchy is of later dating. In the *Rg Veda* (VIII, 31) "we read of the couple (*dampati*, householder and housewife) that "extracts the soma with their minds united in harmony cleans it and mixes it with milk" and makes worship to the gods".[311]

But from whence comes caste? The *Atharvaveda* talks of the four castes—*Brahmans, Kshatriyas, Vaiśyas and Sūdras* where the Brahmans take godly forms.[312] Likewise the *Brāhmanas*, not only theorized on caste, but "exceeded all limits".[313] In the Iranian tradition the king of kings (*Shāhān Shāh-ī-Ērān*) was a messianic form of personification of all the social formations. He was priest, warrior, peasant and artisan all at the same time. But he is not a combination of all classes in the Indian narrative. Caste thus with its ideology of purity and pollution is basically an Indian phenomenon, though its echoes are heard elsewhere too. Its rationale is justified in its "Books", from the *Atharavaveda* to the *Brāhmanas, Puranas* and the *Dharmashastras*. In this sense Partha Chatterjee is wrong when he says that caste is based only on power and not on religion and belief in the supernatural along with rituals.[314] What Chatterjee does not understand is that ritual is itself a vehicle for power. For it rationalizes not only the most de-humanized division of labour between physical labour that was said to be unclean; and mental labour, but also rationalizes the division between people, as the difference beytwen "pure people" and "polluted people".

With British colonialism and the coming of capital, caste took a different form. It did not die out. The teleological argument that capitalism is relatively "progressive" cannot give to the ethical argument that caste would wither away with the coming of capitalism and liberal democracy. Instead what we see is that capital and liberalism would fashion caste according to their images. This itself, leads to the question: What is the Indian mode of production? Because of direct British colonial rule in India; rule that Marx called "futile and actually stupid",[315] we had not merely a "hybrid" mode of production, but what one could call a "caricatured" mode of production. Capitalism that would develop in India would be caricatured capitalism. The new classes that developed with Cornwallis' Permanent Settlement Act, especially the landlords would not be either the English type landlords, or the South Asian variety. They would be caricatures of the English. Consider Marx:

> In Bengal they created a caricature of English large-scale landed property; in the southeast they created a caricature of peasant landholdings. In the northwest they did all they could to transform the Indian economic community with community ownership of the soil into a caricature of itself.[316]

To conclude it is important to point out that pre-capitalism has at least two different forms:

1. Asian community form, and
2. West European small peasant form.[317]

One cannot collapse one into the other, nor read Asian history into the text of Eurocentrism. Consequently it is important to understand that "Marx had examined the different course that these (historical) developments had taken place in Asia as opposed to Western Europe."[318] And because of this difference, that caste grew from the Indic variation of the Asiatic mode. The problem is that due to the neurotic structure of caste—one abolishes it only to make it reappear once again—caste could not be abolished. And with this uncanny and neurotic return of caste, appeared too the "despot" as the head and manager of this awful system.

And under the liberal democratic project of affirmation of caste, we have not only developed a system of schizophrenic racism, we have all become schizophrenic racists. The despot is not an Oriental despot, he is a schizophrenic despot.

To Recreate Dialectical and Historical Materialism

The primary question is not to develop a "sociology of caste", but to recall once again dialectical and historical materialism, but purged from the counterrevolutionary hijacking of the same by the Stalinists. This is done by the phenomenology of humanism. Humanism is the basis of the dialectic. Probably one of the greatest errors in Marxism, in order to be "scientific", has tried to create a full proof "system", never mind that this form of system, as Engels informed us, is necessarily metaphysical.[319] "For it" (meaning the dialectical method), as Engels says, "nothing is final, absolute, sacred. It reveals the transitory character of everything and in everything; nothing can endure before it except the uninterrupted process of becoming and of passing away, of endless ascendancy from the lower to the higher".[320]

What this so-called "full proof system" did was that it objectified itself in such a way that it erased humanity from this very system itself. We got therefore a system without humanity, or to borrow the language of the structuralists we had a *structure without the subject*. Althusser's "theoretical anti-humanism" would be the logical consequence of this.[321] Consider Althusser:

> So any thought that appeals to Marx for any kind of restoration of theological anthropology or humanism is no more than ashes, theoretically. But in practice it could pile up a monument of pre-Marxist ideology that would weigh down on real history and threaten to lead it into blind alleys.[322]

I had said in articles in *Mainstream* and later in *Why We Are Not Hindus* that humanism is central to Marxism and Marxism cannot merely be defined as dialectical and historical materialism, but as *dialectical and historical-humanist materialism*. My contention is that one cannot locate the questions of caste, its relation to the modern class system and capital accumulation, when one operates with the fallacious question of understanding history as unilinear history. It must be noted that this view of history as the march-past of "iron laws" that run independent of humanity was part of the discourse of the Second International. The fact that it was then canonized by Stalin and then converted to gospel truth seems to be ignored by even the most serious social scientists studying caste. Recall that this misinterpretation of Marx was based on the theory of inevitability of historical "happenings" based itself on the almost conscious ignorance of Marx's *Economic and Philosophic Manuscripts of 1844* and the *Ethnological Notebooks* where human agency and the philosophy of praxis are central to philosophical repertoire. The fact that Marx almost never used the term *unvermeidliche* (or "ineveitable") and that it was an almost unwitting inclusion by Engels seems totally forgotten by social science. Recall Marx's humanist understanding of history which I keep at the core of Marxist repertoire: "*History* does *nothing*, it 'possesses no immense wealth', it 'wages *no* battles'. It is the *human*, real, living humanity who does all that...."[323]

It is in this new epistemic space that we claim that the classical understanding of Marxism as dialectical and humanist materialism needs to be rethought as *dialectical and historical-humanist materialism*. What does this mean? What does humanism do in the text of dialectical and historical materialism? According to the dialectic of history we have "the estrangement of the human essence" (*der Entfremdung des menschlichen Wesens*)[324] and "the transcendence of the estrangement" (*die Aufhebung der Entfremdung*)[325] which is also defined as "the appropriation of the human essence" (*die Aneignung des menschlichen Wesens*).[326]

It is this humanist dialectic that one needs to grasp where we have the "form of estrangement" (*Form der Entfremdung*)[327] which now crystallized as an "alien reality" (*Fremde Wirklichkeit*)[328] overcomes human reality and makes history appear as something alien and beyond their control. We must keep this phenomenology of alienation and the struggle to overcome it at the base of the dialectics of history. Besides this also look into another humanist idea of Marx's politics:

> Equality, is nothing but a translation of the German "Ich=Ich" into the French, i.e. political form. Equality as the basis of communism is its *political* justification, and it is the same when the German justifies it by conceiving humanity as *universal self-consciousness*.[329]

It is in this very space that one locates both Marx's humanism as well as the positivist understanding of history that Indian Marxists of the most serious caliber from E.M.S. Namboodripad, Kosambi to R.S. Sharma and Irfan Habib fell prey to. The fact that Marx's *Economic and Philosophic Manuscripts of 1844* and the *Ethnological Notebooks* are absent from their theoretical repertoire needs being stressed. The fact that even Gramsci and Lukács are absent not to forget Raya Dunayevskaya needs also to be restressed. What one needs to do is link Marxism as historicism and humanism with both the problematic of alienation as well as with the idea of multilinear historicism.

What we need to do is to talk of the caste system as an "alien being" (*fremden Wesen*)[330] which has an "alien power".[331] While Marx's *Economic and Philosophic Manuscripts of 1844* is seen as referring to the problematic of alienation in capitalist society, the reference of this problematic to the caste system has hitherto not been explored. It is only with this alien machine that the Caste Overlords can rule over the masses. It is in this way that we transcribe the ideas of "alien reality (*fremde Wirklichkeit*)[332] with its "estranged form" (*entfremdete Gestalt*)[333] into the study of the caste system. Consequently it is with this idea of the "form of estrangement" (*Form der Entfremdung*)[334] that we relate not only to Marx's idea of the metamorphosis of commodities, but also to the metamorphosis of humanity under the caste system.

In this sense we transcend theories of caste from Herbert Risley to Louis Dumont and Nicholas Dirks. What we are saying is that a mere sociology of caste is not enough to have a scientific understanding of the same. The dialectics of history and the phenomenology of alienation are important to uncover the very mechanism of the caste system.

Unfortunately the Left in India has not taken caste at all in their mode of inquiry, forget taking caste in the philosophical sense that we just outlined. Instead it jumped directly into bourgeois legality and hailed the parliament and also what Marx calls "parliamentary cretinism".[335] The Left forgot that they would also be reduced to cretinism.

Mistake of the Stalinists and the Postmodernists

To sum up we claim again that the main mistake is that which Edward Said made in thinking that the Asiatic mode of production was an Orientalist intervention and Marx became a Romantic and Messianic Orientalist condemning non-European societies to eternal backwardness[336]. This idea is completely wrong. It must be noted that Lawrence Krader took out Marx's unpublished Notebooks at the same time as Said's *Orientalism*. Any coincidence?

But what is forgotten is that besides the use of the method of Michel Foucault by Edward Said (in castigating the idea of the Asiatic mode of production) was the brutality of Stalinism in deciding the fate of the idea of the Asiatic mode of production. Neither was the Soviet historian S. Shmonin, who advocated the idea of the Asiatic mode in 1929, ever referred to, nor was Plekhanov's *History of Russian Social Thought* taken seriously. What has to be noted is that by 1931 there were no references to this mode in discussions in the Soviet Union. Not only was the discussion under Stalin purged—M.D. Kokin, the Soviet proponent of this idea, died in the Stalinist anti-communist genocide—but even Marxist scholars like G.A. Cohen, Maurice Dobb and Paul Sweezy made no reference to it. Moreover Harbans Mukhia's 'Was There Feudalism in Indian History?'[337] was not taken as seriously.

To once more sum up our argument we say that repercussion of this theme of ignoring the Asiatic mode of production is that the history of the world was made to look like a form of "mono-history" where the discourse of the infamous march-past of iron laws governed human reasoning. According to this thesis capitalism could only emerge from feudalism, while communism could only grow from capitalism. There could be no alternative for the emergence of communism. And since India is not capitalist (or not "fully developed" capitalist), communism would have to wait for the missing messiah to redeem India.

But there are other views that we must mention, namely those of Kevin Anderson wherein he states that capitalism emerged in India not from feudalism, but from primitive commune property.[338] Strangely because of the hegemony of this "mono-historical" narrative, it would be a form of anarchism that would attempt to seek an alternative path. And anarchism in the form of the Indian Maoists took up the view of tribal commune property—the *ager publicus* (public lands) of Marx's *Pre-capitalist Economic Formations*—as the pivotal force for the Indian revolution. But here anarchism of the Indian Maoists would end when they would succumb to the theory of the New Democratic Revolution that would also state the inevitability of capitalism. This theory of the inevitability of capitalism would claim that communism can only emerge from capitalism. Little would they know that the old thesis of semi-feudalism and the New Democratic Revolution will be the rocks to which Indian anarchists would be permanently chained. Neither the Parliamentary Left nor the Maoists have ever thought that communism in India can come directly by simply skipping over capitalism.

In this perspective of multilinear historicism one recalls Marx's phrase that just as the history of the expropriation of the peasantry "in different countries, assumes different aspects", so too the emergence of the modern proletariat takes different forms.[339] And since it was only in England that took what Marx calls the "classical form",[340] one cannot remain enslaved only to this European form of capitalism. What one needs to tell the Indian comrades is that one need not *pass through the dreadful vicissitudes of capitalism.*[341]

That the articulation of the Parliamentary Left (along with the Indian anarchist Maoists) who want to march with the myth of historical inevitabilities is in direct opposition to Marx's formulation of *jumps in history* determined by the radical politics of permanent revolution also ought to be noted. They seem to have forgotten that the "historical inevitability" of the rise of capitalism that involves the divorcing of the producer from the means of production was limited only to Western Europe.[342] One cannot impose this history onto the entire world. As Marx said with reference to another Narodniki, Mikhailowsky, there is no "general path of development prescribed by fate to all nations" where one could impose a "general historico-philosophical theory" onto the entire world.[343] Recall Marx again "the supreme virtue of this (understanding) consists in being supra-historical".[344]

Negating Stalinism and Postmodernism

The categorical imperative is to negate both Stalinism as well as postmodernity to look anew into the caste question embedded in the Asiatic mode of production. What I am doing is keeping this very important theme of multilinearism in mind, whereby one is able to locate the complexity of Indian history. One is also able to see how Indian history keeps its pre-capitalist formations within its capitalist breast and thus hops on its two feet—one being the archaic caste foot, the other the modern class foot. And because the caste foot is ahead of the class foot one can say that one "suffers not only from the development of capitalist production, but also from the incompleteness of that development".[345] The tragedy of Indian history is that it shall be haunted not merely by the incompleteness of bourgeois development, but by the impossibility of this alleged "full development". It is in the womb of this underdevelopment that one reads Marx's viewing of the Oriental state as the *"despotic" sovereign*, along with the village communities that are said to be "contaminated by caste and slavery".[346] At one level, the caste system seems to echo Marx's views of feudal Europe stuck with its idiocy and superstition. At another level it is concrete and anticipates Ambedkar's critique of the caste system where caste not only degrades and saps the energies of the peasants and the menial castes, but degrades humanity as a whole.

We thus reemphasize the articulation of caste in India and the imperative to theorize on this peculiar phenomenon from a non-essentialist historical materialist problematic. In this sense it is in contrast to thinkers in the genre of not only the Stalinists, not only in the problematic of Edward Said and his postmodern followers, but also against the giants of contemporary social science, namely, Louis Dumont and Nicholas Dirks. So is Habib correct in stating that caste is the "Western sociologist's image"[347] of Indian society? Further is Dirks correct when he says that caste is a "modern" phenomenon and a colonial construct to manage and govern the Eastern frontiers of the British Empire? Is he correct in saying that caste is a "peculiar form of modern Western nostalgia"?[348] For Dirks caste as a "central symbol" of Indian civilization[349] entirely misses the point both of the colonial narrative and the political economy of imperialism. If it was the British that reified caste, as Dirks suggests[350], then the reading of caste had to change, a change that would directly challenge not only the understanding of caste from Hegel and Weber to Dumont, but also challenge Ambedkar's radical thesis.[351] Dirks' epistemic repertoire is, as must be pointed out, borrowed from Michel Foucault and Edward Said. Consider Dirks:

> ...why is it that caste has become for so many the core symbol of community in India, wherein for others, even in serious critique, caste is still the defining feature of Indian social organization....Caste, as we know it today, is not in fact some unchanged survival of ancient India, not some single system that reflects a core civilizational value, not an expression of Indian tradition. Rather, I will argue that caste (again as we know it today) is a modern phenomenon, that it is, specifically, the product of an historical encounter between India and Western colonial rule. By this I do not mean to imply that it was simply invented by the too clever British, now credited with so many imperial patents that what began as a colonial critique has turned into another form of imperial domination. But I am suggesting that under the British that "caste" became a single term capable of expressing, organizing, and above all "systematizing" India's diverse forms of social identity, community and organization. This was achieved through an identifiable (if contested) ideological canon as the result of a concrete encounter with colonial modernity during two hundred years of Bristish domination. In short, colonialism made caste what it is today. It made the conditions that made possible..(of) making caste the central symbol of Indian society.[352]

In this space one raises the question: If caste is merely a colonial invention (even as "caste as we know it") devoid of its pre-capitalist genealogy, then would not the Dirks-inspired thesis also fall in the same trap of not sufficiently studying pre-capitalist India? If the Indian Left historians from Sharma to Habib erred in mentioning an "Indian feudalism", Dirks would not even talk of that. Foucault's spectre would not allow this. Yes he does talk of "colonial feudalism" and "feudal politics".[353] Unlike the Left historians there is no serious idea of feudalism itself. Further:

> The idea that *varna*—the classification of all castes into four hierarchical orders with the Brahman on top—could conceivably organize the social identities and relations of all Indians across the civilizational expanse of the subcontinent was only developed under the peculiar circumstances of British colonial rule.[354]

But then how does one read Albêrûnî's eleventh century idea of "castes called "colours" (*Varna*) and on the classes below them"?[355] Would Dirks also situate this in the colonial context? Was Albêrûnî a colonial modernist? What is this ideology of prevention of "intermixture and disorder" that clearly arises in Manu's law, the one that *The Gita* keeps central to the horrors of caste intermixture and the one that Albêrûnî notes?[356] So where stands Dirks' idea that "caste was not a single category or even a single logic of categorization, even for Brahmans, who were the primary beneficiaries of the caste idea"?[357] But then note once again Albêrûnî on sin and the "transgression of the rule" of breaking caste law, a noting that is diametrically opposite of Dirks' thesis.[358]

We will have to insist that we need a deeper sense of history whereby one can create new theories, than merely creating abstract a-historical theories. Dirks' statement that "caste has always been political"[359] says almost nothing at all. If there is the production of abstract theories, we also have the muttering of angry statements. The Established Left (now joined by Arvind Kejriwal) is an example of merely muttering angry statements. The Established Left like the traditional Ambedkarites act according to the reactive principle, forgetting that there is a radical distinction between the reactive force and the active force.

But this would primarily require the abolition of the old type of thinking. It must be said that for emancipatory politics (as I noted earlier), it is not that fascism is the biggest threat. It is liberalism that has always been the biggest threat since it involves what Žižek calls the *Denkverbot* or the "prohibitions against thinking". *Fascism is merely liberalism that has gone haywire.* Liberalism is not the other face of fascism. It is most certainly not the antidote to fascism.

The Established Left has for long been the spokesperson of the Congress. But has the Congress done anything good for the downtrodden? Here it is important to recall Ambedkar:

> Had the Untouchables gone over to the Congress? Such a thing was to me unimaginable. For I could not believe that the Untouchables—apart from a few agents of the Congress who are always tempted by the Congress gold to play the part of the traitor—could think of going over to the Congress en masse forgetting how Mr. Gandhi and the Congress opposed, inch by inch up to the very last moment, every one of their demands for political safeguards.[360]

One must note that it was the Congress led by Gandhi since the 1920s that sabotaged the democratic movement in India. One must note that Gandhi always wanted to "manage" caste. He needed caste in order to be its Chief Manager. After independence it was the Western educated Nehru who became the manager. Unlike Gandhi whose ideology was essentially backward looking and reactionary (as Perry Anderson rightly notes in his *The Indian Ideology*), Nehru brought in the discourses of progress, secularism and socialism in the national mainstream. In the early 1990s, it was the followers of Nehru—Narasimha Rao and Manmohan Singh—who started the burial of secularism and Nehruvian socialism. And with 2014 we must recognize that the liberal project is completely dead. We cannot fool ourselves (like the Established Left led by the CPI(M) is trying to do) that dead liberalism can come alive again.

And since global capital funds not only the Indian liberals led by the Congress as also the neo-cons and communal-fascists, one will have to actively transcend the liberal and neo-con imagination for a Revolutionary Internationalism where the smashing of caste is inexorably linked to the smashing of capitalism and imperialism. From henceforth the Asian Soviets will have to replace the traditional Dalit and Left parties. The annihilation of caste will require the annihilation of feudo-capitalist bureaucracies not only in India, but in the entire South Asian region, thus directly fighting against the militarization of this region which is keeping the capitalist and caste-clan system alive.

Revolutionary Internationalism will have to widen the scope of freedom struggles. Not only will the freedom of labour (free from capital), but also freedom from caste and patriarchy as also freedom of oppressed nationalities, thus freedom of all humanity will have to be written on the banners of the Revolutionary Left. The space that we need to create is a much larger space, thus freeing ourselves from colonial cartography and nationalist imagination created by the colonialists aided by Gandhi and Nehru, Savarkar and Golwalkar.

But this will imply awakening from the spell of the dream that we are told is true. For that one will also have to recreate the idea of the spectre of communism that will haunt the global bourgeoisie. Old Ontology will have to be replaced by a New Ontology. The name of this New Ontology will be hauntology to be precise. The *Manifesto of the Communist Party* will have to be relived. The arena of the struggle against caste is much wider than imagined in the fantasyland of the Indian parliament. It requires another space. It also requires struggles unimaginable for the legal Marxists and traditional Ambedkarites who merely mutter angry statements in parliament.

The questions remain: *Are the present comrades ready for this? Will they be prepared to think for themselves? Will they dare to remove the locks kept on their minds by the party elites? Will they cease being blinded by the silence of the elites? Will they see and hear for themselves? Or will silent blindness devour them completely where they would scream*:

> Should this torture then torment us
> Since it brings us greater pleasure?
> Were not through the rule of Timur
> Souls devoured without measure?

Conclusion: Souls Devoured without Measure

In the *Economic and Philosophic Manuscripts of 1844* Marx quotes Shakespeare:

> …beasts
> May have the world in empire![361]

The empire has come and it is the beast who is ruling. Our Left bereft of all scientific reasoning, sought a Revolution without a Revolution. They got one. The only thing is that this revolutionary who now wears the crown of the revolutionary is in actuality the fascist. The Indian Left comprises *duplicate* revolutionaries. But what they gave birth to was the *real* fascist. They now try to hide in the parliament, but they do not see the fascists tearing down the very same parliament. The only possible redemption for then is the Maoists whom they both feared and loathed, these anarcho-terrorists who are nothing but *Stalinists in rebellion against Stalinism.*

So one may ask: If the Established Left has destroyed the very idea of universal emancipation, and if fascism and Stalinism have triumphed, is Leninism dead? One recalls Žižek here:

> The dead Lenin who does not know that he is dead thus stands for our own obstinate refusal to renounce the grandiose Utopian projects and accept the limitations of our situation: there is no big Other, Lenin was mortal and made errors like others, so it is time for us to let him die, to put to rest this obscene ghost which haunts our political imaginary, and to approach our problems in a non-ideological and pragmatic way. But there is another sense in which Lenin is still alive: he is alive in which he embodies what Badiou calls 'the eternal Idea' of universal emancipation, the immortal striving for justice that no insult or catastrophe managed to kill.[362]

For the Indian Established Left now married to the parliament and the classes that control the parliament, the question of liberal ideology is of utmost importance. For them there is no question of dialectics, no question of the dialectics of negation that Marx celebrated throughout his life. The questions of dialectical materialism and that of the dictatorship of the proletariat are simply out of the question.

Liberalism enchants the entire world with its fake promises. It lives in the world of pure appearances, in fact fetishized appearances that veil class reality. In contrast, Marx in the third volume of *Capital*, says that the stripping of the "estranged outward appearance of economic relationships" forms the basis of the dialectical materialist method.[363] Marx adds: "All science would be superfluous if the outward appearance and the essence of things directly coincided"[364] and that the "force of abstraction" would serve as the microscope that would be able to discover the "economic-cell form" of society.[365] What is thus needed is the "microscopic anatomy" of society.[366] In the *Economic and Philosophic Manuscripts of 1844* Marx had talked of:

> The outstanding achievement of Hegel's *Phänomenologie* and of its final outcome, the dialectic of negativity as the moving and generating principle, is thus first that Hegel conceives the self-creation of man as a process, conceives objectification as loss of the object, as alienation and as transcendence of this alienation; that he thus grasps the essence of *labour* and comprehends objective humanity—true, because real human—as the outcome of humanity's *own labour*. The *real, active* orientation of humanity to itself as a species-being, or its manifestation as a real species-being (i.e. as a human being), is only possible if humanity really brings out all its *species-powers*—something which in turn is only possible through the cooperative action of all of humankind, only as the result of history—and treats these powers as objects: and this, to begin with, is again only possible in the form of estrangement.[367]

What happens in this state of estrangement is the transfiguration and glorification of the existing state of things. What the world bourgeois does not notice is that the "crisis is once again approaching, although as yet but in its preliminary stage".[368] But because of the "universality of its theatre and the intensity of its action", to recall good old Marx once again, it will drum dialectics even into the heads of the mushroom-upstarts of the not so new, holy capitalist empire.[369]

The 1980s saw the emergence of Reaganism and the brutal supremacy of American militarism and Machiavellian policy which trapped the Soviets in Afghanistan and led them to their "inevitable" grave. While Ronald Reagan was seen in the picture as the gravedigger, the figure of Stalin can also be seen in the burial ground of communism. Now we live in the post-Reagan era of Donald Trump where even the "moral confidence" (to use a term of William Kristol and Robert Kagan) of American imperialism has given way to crass brutality. This world of crass brutality has also transcended the Bush policy of the "war on terror". Trump's crass brutality is the New Terror of imperialism. It is this Not So Brave New World of the New

Terror of Imperialism that one asks the very simple question: How is revolution possible?

It is Engels who had once said that:

> The ruling big bourgeoisie has fulfilled its historical mission (*Beruf*), that it is no longer capable of the leadership of society and has even become a hindrance to the development of production....that historical leadership (*Leitung*) has passed to the proletariat, a class which, owing to its position in society, can free itself by abolishing altogether class rule, all servitude and all exploitation.[370]

To counter revolutionary action, fascism has created its own version of alleged "radicality". Fascism had created its own form of messianic character to counter Marxism with its idea of pseudo-rebellion. In 1928 Joseph Goebbels, the Nazi minister of propaganda wrote in *Der Angrifff*:

> We go into the Reichstag in order to acquire the weapons of democracy from its arsenal. We become Reichstag deputies in order to paralyze the Weimar democracy with its own assistance. If democracy is stupid enough to give us free travel privileges and per diem allowances for this service, that is its affair......We come as enemies! Like the wolf tearing into the flock of sheep that is how we have come.[371]

Indeed, the wolves have come. But then are we sheep? How do we counter the wolves? It is simple: by going to the masses, living with them, learning from them. And this is what Marxist-Humanism really means. Marxist-Humanism is in this sense revolutionary. But then it is at the same time scientific. "To write poetry after Auschwitz is barbaric".[372] We know this for sure. In this case what does one do with Goethe? Should we forget him? Should we drown in this crisis, these multiple crises, where humanity itself is now in a state of crisis?

Yes the crisis has once again come. But instead of seeing Lenin and the Bolsheviks in this familiar scene of action, we see the hosts and the ghosts of the world counterrevolution. Of course Reagan is around, but now appearing in the form of Donald Trump. But the most dreadful thing is that in Lenin's empty seat, we see once again the figure of Stalin.

Zuleika died and has to die once again. Stalin killed her. Stalin's ghost will continue to destroy all memories of her. Instead of the torture of the love of Zuleika for Yusuf which ought to have tormented us, we are tormented by the raid of Timur. Everyone has become Timur. Consequently we hear once again the cry of the German bard:

Should this torture then torment us
Since it brings us greater pleasure?
Were not through the rule of Timur
Souls devoured without measure?

References & Notes

1. See 'Genesis', 39:6. See also Sura 12 'Josef', in *The Koran*, trans. J.M. Rodwell (London: J.M. Dent & Sons Ltd., 1983), p. 232 for the Islamic rendering of the narrative of the seduction of Yusuf by Zuleika.
2. Erich Fromm, 'The Male Creation', in *Love, Sexuality and Matriarchy: About Gender* (New York: Fromm International Publishing Corporation, 1997), p. 51.
3. Johann Wolfgang von Goethe, 'Zuleika Speaks', in *West-East Divan*, trans. Martin Bidney (New York: State University of New York Press, 2010), p. 52.
4. Johann Wolfgang von Goethe, 'Invitation', in Ibid., p. 87.
5. Karl Marx, 'The British Rule in India', in *Marx. Engels. On Colonialism* (Moscow: Progress Publishers, 1976), p. 41.
6. See my *In the Name of Marx* (Delhi: Aakar Books, 2018).
7. Karl Marx, 'Revelations of the Diplomatic History of the 18th Century', in *Marx. Engels. Collected Works*, Vol. 15 (Moscow: Progress Publishers, 1986), p. 77.
8. Ibid., p. 87.
9. See Peter Hudis's *Marx's Concept of the Alternative to Capitalism* (Delhi: Aakar Books, 2016).
10. V.I. Lenin, 'Letter to the Congress, December 23, 1922', in *V.I. Lenin. Selected Works* (Moscow: Progress Publishers, 1977), p. 675.
11. Ibid., p. 676.
12. Slavoj Žižek, 'Foreword to Trotsky. Terrorism and Communism, or, Despair and Utopia in the Turbulent Years of 1920', in *Slavoj*

Žižek Presents Trotsky. Terrorism and Communism (London: Verso, 2007), p. XIX.

13. See Harold R. Isaacs, *The Tragedy of the Chinese Revolution* (Stanford University Press, 1961), p. 162.
14. See Leon Trotsky, 'The Chinese Revolution and the Theses of Comrade Stalin', May 7, 1927, in *The Hidden Dynamics of Chinese Revolution. Writings and Speeches of Leon Trotsky on China (1925-1940)*, ed. Rajesh Tyagi (Delhi: Aakar Books, 2009), p. 153.
15. Ibid.
16. Ibid., pp. 153-4.
17. Ibid., p. 155.
18. Ibid., p. 156.
19. Leon Trotsky, 'The Friendly Exchange of Portraits Between Stalin and Chiang Kai-shek', April 18, 1927 in ibid., p. 145.
20. Ibid.
21. Ibid.
22. Leon Trotsky, 'On the Slogan of Soviets in China', April 16, 1927, in ibid., p. 137.
23. J.V. Stalin, 'Economic Problems of Socialism in the USSR', in *J.V. Stalin. Selected Writings*, Vol. II (Calcutta: National Book Agency, 1976), pp. 288-89
24. Ibid.
25. Karl Marx, 'Theses on Feuerbach', in *Marx. Engels. Selected Works* (Moscow: Progress Publishers, 1975), p. 28.
26. Ibid.
27. Ibid.
28. Ibid., p. 30.
29. See my *In the Name of Marx* (Delhi: Aakar Books, 2018), p. 89.
30. Karl Marx, 'The Eighteenth Brumaire of Louis Bonaparte', in *Marx. Engels. Selected Works* (Moscow: Progress Publishers, 1975), p. 96.
31. Slavoj Žižek, op. cit, p. XX.
32. Ibid., p. XXXII.
33. Joseph Hansen, 'Forward' to Leon Trotsky's *Stalin's Frame-up System and The Moscow Trials* (New York: Pioneer Publishers, 1950), p. XI.
34. Mussolini, *Popolo d'Ttalia*, quoted in ibid.

35. Sydney Hook, *Out of Step: An Unquiet Life in the 20th Century* (New York: Caroll & Grat, 1988).

36. V.I. Lenin, 'On the Establishment of the U.S.S.R. Letter to L.B. Kamevev. For Members of the Political Bureau, C.C. R.C.P. (B)', in *V.I. Lenin. Selected Works in Three Volumes,* Vol. 3 (Moscow: Progress Publishers, 1977), p. 651.

37. V.I. Lenin, 'The Question of Nationalities or "Autonomization"', in *V.I. Lenin. Selected Works in Three Volumes,* Vol. 3, p. 689.

38. Ibid.

39. Ibid., pp. 690-1.

40. Isaac Deutscher, *The Prophet Armed. Trotsky: 1879-1921* (New York: Oxford University Press, 1954), p. 458.

41. V.I. Lenin, op. cit., p. 691.

42. Isaac Deutscher, op. cit., p. 405.

43. Ibid.

44. Mikhail Bulgakov, 'Prospects for the Future', Article Published in the Local Newspaper of the Town of Gronzy, in the Northern Caucasus, November 26, 1919, in J.A.E. Curtis, *Manuscripts Don't Burn. Mikhail Bulgakov: A Life in Letters and Diaries* (London: Bloomsbury Publishing Ltd., 2012), p. 16.

45. Ibid., p. 17.

46. Ibid.

47. Ibid.

48. Ibid.

49. Herbert Marcuse, 'To Heidegger', August 28, 1947, in *Herbert Marcuse, Technology, War and Fascism. Collected Papers of Herbert Marcuse,* Vol. One (London: Routledge, 1998), p. 263.

50. Ibid., p. 264.

51. Martin Heidegger, 'To Marcuse', January 20, 1948, in ibid., p. 265.

52. See Karl Marx and Frederick Engels, 'Manifesto of the Communist Party', in *Marx. Engels. Selected Works* (Moscow: Progress Publishers, 1975), p. 35.

53. See John Dewey, *Later Works, 1925-53, Vol. II, 1935-37,* ed. Jo Ann-Boydston (Carbondale: Southern Illinois University Press, 2008).

54. For fascism and Nazism, communism was a product of the "Jewish conspiracy" and the Jews from Marx to Trotsky were

out to destroy the good Christian world built on private property and redemption from Original Sin. For the global right-wing, from Europe and USA to Iran, Pakistan and India, communism is a "disease" and "danger". The "disease" (according to Bulgakov) and "danger" (according to Heidegger) of communism became a deadly irreligious spectre respecting neither religion, national borders nor private property. For Stalin, likewise, Trotsky was the "Wandering Jew" who instead of attempting to build "socialism in one country" (like the Jew devoid of national sentiments) wanted to export revolutions worldwide. For the elites one has to exorcize this ghost before it sends all of us into eternal damnation. In Europe it would be Stalin and Hitler who would save both Russia and Western Dasein against the vermin spread by Trotsky. In India it would be someone else who would save Indian from this terrible spectre.

55. Perry Anderson, *The Indian Ideology* (Gurgaon: Three Essays Collective, 2012), p. 18, n. 16.
56. B.R. Ambedkar, 'Reply to the Mahatma', in *The Essential Writings of B.R. Ambedkar*, ed. Valerian Rodrigues (New Delhi: Oxford University Press, 2008), p. 318.
57. Perry Anderson, op. cit., p. 18.
58. George Orwell, 'Reflections on Gandhi', first published: *Partisan Review*, London, January 1949 in http://www.orwell.ru/library/reviews/gandhi/english/e_gandhi.
59. 2014 saw the right-wing Hindu nationalist party Bharatiya Janata Party come to power while in 2017 Donald Trump became the President of the USA.
60. Leon Trotsky, 'An Open Letter to the Workers of India', (July 1939), in *New Wave*, September, 2010.
61. Karl Marx, 'Address to the Central Committee of the Communist League', in *Marx. Engels. Selected Works in Three Volumes*, Volume Three (Moscow: Progress Publishers, 1977), p. 177.
62. Ibid.
63. Ibid., p. 177.
64. V.I. Lenin, 'The Historical Destiny of the Doctrine of Karl Marx', in *V.I. Lenin. Selected Works* (Moscow: Progress Publishers, 1977), p. 19.
65. Ibid., p. 18.

66. Ibid., p. 19.
67. Leon Trotsky, 'An Open Letter to the Workers of the World', July, 1939, in *New Wave*, September, 2010.
68. Ibid.
69. Georgi Dimitrov, 'The Fascist Offensive and the Tasks of the Communist International,' in *VII Congress of the Communist International: Abridged Stenographic Report of Proceedings*, (Moscow: Foreign Languages Publishing House, 1939), p. 126.
70. See my *In the Name of Marx*, p. 57.
71. Slavoj Žižek, 'Introduction. Robespierre, or the 'Divine Violence' of Terror', in Maximilien Robespierre, *Virtue and Terror* (London: Verso, 2007), pp. VII-VIII.
72. Ibid., pp. VII. Robespierre 'On the Principles of Political Morality that Should Guide the National Convention in the Domestic Administration of the Republic', in ibid., p. 115. The quote is of Robespierre.
73. See Karl Marx, 'Letter to the Editorial Board of the *Otechestevenniye Zapiski*, November 1877', in *Marx. Engels. Selected Correspondence* (Moscow: Progress Publishers, 1975); and Karl Marx, 'First Draft of the Reply to V.I. Zasulich's Letter', in *Marx Engels. Selected Works*, Volume Three (Moscow; Progress Publishers, 1970). See also Karl Marx and Frederick Engels, 'Preface to the Second Edition' of the *Manifesto of the Communist Party'*, in Theodor Shanin (ed). *Late Marx and the Russian Road. Marx and the Peripheries of Capitalism* (Delhi: Aakar Books 2009), p. 139, where Marx talks of a direct jump from pre-capitalism to socialism and how the Russian Revolution and the proletarian revolutions in advanced capitalist nations have to complement one another. Here Marx's internationalism is obvious. All revolutions are global revolutions and occur simultaneously.
74. Prabhat, Patnaik, 'E.M.S. Namboodiripad's Perception of History', in *The Marxist*, XXV, 3-4 July-September, 2009, pp. 5-6 which I had included in my *Challenges for the Indian Left*.
75. Anand Teltumbde, *The Persistence of Caste* (New Delhi: Navayana Press, 2010).
76. See Rosa Luxemburg, 'The Accumulation of Capital—An Anti-Critique', in Rosa Luxemburg and Nicolai Bukharin, *Imperialism and the Accumulation of Capital*, trans. Rudolf Wichmann (London: Allen Lane, The Penguin Press, 1972), pp. 61-2, 77.

77. Karl Marx, *Capital,* Vol. I trans. Samuel Moore and Edward Aveling (Moscow: Progress Publishers), 1983, p. 19
78. Karl Marx, 'To Frederick Engels, in London' Manchester, June 6, 1853, in *Marx. Engels. Selected Correspondence* (Moscow: Progress Publishers, 1975), p. 80.
79. Karl Marx, 'The British Rule in India', in *Marx. Engels. On Colonialism* (Moscow: Progress Publishers, 1976), p. 40.
80. Jawaharlal Nehru, *The Discovery of India* (London: Meridian Books Ltd., 1946), pp. 206-212.
81. B.R. Ambedkar, 'Castes in India, their Mechanism, Genesis and Development', in *The Essential Writings of B.R. Ambedkar,* ed. Valerian Rodrigues (New Delhi: Oxford University Press, 2008), pp. 253, 257.
82. Jawaharlal Nehru, op. cit., p. 207.
83. Ibid.
84. Jawaharlal Nehru, *An Autobiography* (New Delhi: Oxford University Press, 2001), p. 13.
85. Perry Anderson, *The Indian Ideology* (Gurgaon: Three Essays Collective, 2012), pp. 19-20.
86. Jawaharlal Nehru, op. cit., p. 15.
87. Ibid.
88. Ibid.
89. Frederick Engels, 'To Conrad Schmidt in Berlin', London, October 27, 1890, in *Marx. Engels. Selected Works* (Moscow: Progress Publishers, 1975), p. 689.
90. Ibid., p. 687.
91. M.K. Gandhi, 'The Caste System' (1920) in *Collected Works of Mahatma Gandhi,* Vol. 19 (Ahmedabad: The Publication Division, Ministry of Information and Broadcasting, Government of India, 1966), p. 83. See also Perry Anderson, *The Indian Ideology* (Gurgaon: Three Essays Collective, 2012), p. 37, n. 40.
92. M.K. Gandhi, 'Letter to Hanumantrao', July 17, 1918, in *Collected Works of Mahatma Gandhi,* Vol. 14 (Ahmedabad: The Publication Division, Ministry of Information and Broadcasting, Government of India, 1965), p. 485.
93. M.K. Gandhi, 'Speech at Ras', June 26, 1918 in *The Bombay Chronicle,* July 2, 1918, in *Collected Works of Mahatma Gandhi,* Vol. 14, p. 454.

94. M.K. Gandhi, 'Letter to C.F. Andrews', June 23, 1918, in *Collected Works of Mahatma Gandhi*, Vol. 14, p. 444.

95. M.K. Gandhi, 'Letter to Hanumantrao', July 17, 1918, in ibid., p. 485.

96. M.K. Gandhi, 'Answers to Zamindars' [July 25, 1934], in *The Penguin Gandhi Reader*, ed. Rudrangshu Mukherjee (New Delhi: Penguin Books, 1993), p. 238.

97. Ibid., pp. 238-240.

98. M.K. Gandhi, *The Bhagavad Gita* (Mumbai: Jaico Publishing House, 2017), p. 3.

99. *Dharmasutra*, I, 1, 1, 4-8. Quoted in Maurice Winternitz, *A History of Indian Literature, Vol. One, Introduction, Veda, Epics, Purānas and Tantras*, trans. V. Srinivasa Sarma (Delhi: Motilal Banarasidas Publishers Pvt. Ltd., 1990), p. 60.

100. See B.R. Ambedkar, 'Gandhism' in *The Essential Writings of B.R. Ambedkar*, ed. Valerian Rodrigues (New Delhi: Oxford University Press, 2008), p. 151.

101. M.K. Gandhi, 'Ahmedabad Mill-hands' Strike', Leaflet, No. 12', in *Collected Works of Mahatma Gandhi*, Vol. 14, p. 249.

102. M.K. Gandhi, 'The Caste System' (1920), in *Collected Works of Mahatma Gandhi*, Vol. 19 (Ahmedabad: The Publication Division, Ministry of Information and Broadcasting, Government of India, 1966), p. 84.

103. Karl Marx, *Economic and Philosophic Manuscripts of 1844* (Moscow: Progress Publishers, 1982), p. 129.

104. Karl Marx, 'The British Rule in India', in *Marx. Engels. On Colonialism*, p. 41.

105. B.R. Ambedkar, *Pakistan or the Partition of India* (Bombay, 1946), p. 354.

106. Avtar Singh, 'After Jat Sikh Kills Self Upon Discovering Wife is Dalit, His Brother Refuses to Marry Her' in *Hindustan Times*, June 3, 2017.

107. Karl Marx *Capital*, Vol. I, pp. 338-9.

108. Karl Marx, *Economic and Philosophic Manuscripts of 1844* (Moscow: Progress Publishers, 1982), p. 134; Karl Marx, 'Nationalökonomie und Philosophie', in Karl Marx, *Die Frühschriften* (Berlin: Alfred Kröner Verlag, 1964), p. 271.

109. See my *The Seductions of Karl Marx* (Delhi: Aakar Books, 2010), pp. 42-3, 58-9.

110. Louis Althusser, *For Marx*, trans. Ben Brewster (London: Allen Lane, 1969), pp. 229-30.
111. William Shakespeare, 'Hamlet. Prince of Denmark', in *The Complete Works of William Shakespeare* (London: Henry Pordes, 1983), Act I, Scene I, p. 942.
112. Ibid., Act I, Scene V, p. 948.
113. B.R. Ambedkar, 'Castes in India, Their Mechanism, Genesis and Development', in *The Essential Writings of B.R. Ambedkar*, ed. Valerian Rodrigues (New Delhi: Oxford University Press, 2008).
114. See my *In the Name of Marx*, pp. 38, 97.
115. See B.R. Ambedkar, 'Capitalism, Labour and Brahmanism', in *Thus Spoke Ambedkar*, ed. Bhagwan Das (New Delhi: Navayana, 2010), p. 50.
116. See Ambedkar, 'The Failures of Parliamentary Democracy', in Ibid., p. 48.
117. B.R. Ambedkar, 'Capitalism, Labour and Brahmanism', p. 51.
118. *In the Name of Marx*, pp. 48-9.
119. Kancha Illaiah Shepherd, 'A Call to Left Liberals', in *Indian Express*, October 17, 2017 where he recalls D. Ajit, Han Docnker and Ravi Saxena's 'Corporate Boards in India; Blocked by Caste', in *Economic & Political Weekly*, Vol. XLVII, No. 31, August 11, 2012.
120. Jawaharlal Nehru, *The Discovery of India*, p. 60.
121. Ibid.
122. Ibid., p. 243.
123. Ibid., p. 273.
124. Jawaharlal Nehru, *An Autobiography*, p. 459.
125. Ibid.
126. *In the Name of Marx*, pp. 52-3.
127. Karl Marx, 'The Eighteenth Brumaire of Louis Bonaparte', in *Marx. Engels. Selected Works*, p. 96.
128. Karl Marx, 'Preface to the First German Edition', *Capital*, Vol. I, p. 20.
129. Ibid.
130. Ibid., p. 96.
131. Ibid.

132. B.R. Ambedkar, *Who Were the Shudras?* (Bombay: Thacker and Co. Ltd., 1970), p. XIV.

133. B.R. Ambedkar, *Pakistan or Partition of India* (Bombay, 1946).

134. This what Lenin said when reading Hegel's *Science of Logic* in the midst of imperialist brutality: "It is impossible to understand Marx's *Capital*, and especially its first chapter, without having thoroughly studied and understood the *whole* of Hegel's *Science of Logic*. Consequently half a century later none of the Marxists understood Marx!!" See V.I. Lenin, *Philosophical Notebooks. Collected Works*, Vol. 38 (Moscow: Progress Publishers, 1981), p. 181.

135. See Frederick Engels, 'Letter to F. Mehring in Berlin', London, July 14, 1893, in *Marx. Engels. Selected Works* (Moscow: Progress Publishers, 1975), p. 690.

136. See Ernesto Laclau and Chantal Mouffe, *Hegemony and Socialist Strategy. Towards a Radical Democratic Politics*, trans. Winston Moore and Paul Cammack (London: Verso, 1985), p. 11.

137. Louis Althusser, *Lenin and Philosophy and Other Essays*, trans. Ben Brewster (Delhi: Aakar Books, 2006), p. 22.

138. Christophe Jafferlot, *Dr. Ambedkar and Untouchability. Analysing and Fighting Caste* (Delhi: Permanent Black, 2005), p. 75.

139. Ibid., p. 79.

140. B.R. Ambedkar, *Dr. B.R. Ambedkar. Writings and Speeches*, Vol. 2 (Mumbai: Dr. Babasaheb Ambedkar Source Material Publication Committee, 1982), p. 256.

141. Frederick Engels, 'To C. Schmidt in Berlin', London, August 5, 1890, in *Marx. Engels. Selected Works*, p. 679.

142. See Fredric Jameson, *Postmodernism or the Cultural Logic of Late Capitalism* (London: Verso, 1991), p. 14.

143. M.K. Gandhi, 'The Congress and After', *Young India*, January 5, 1922, in *What is Hinduism?* (New Delhi: National Book Trust, 2011), p. 15.

144. M.K. Gandhi, 'My Mission', *Young India*, April 3, 1924, in ibid., p. 17.

145. Ibid.

146. M.K. Gandhi, 'What May Hindus Do?', in *Young India*, June 19, 1924, in ibid., p. 21.

147. Ibid., pp. 21-2.

148. Fredric Jameson, *Postmodernism or the Cultural Logic of Late Capitalism* (London: Verso, 1991), p. 14.
149. Ibid.
150. Ibid.
151. See Karl Marx and Frederick Engels, *The Holy Family* (Moscow: Progress Publishers, 1980), p. 46.
152. Fredric Jameson, op. cit.
153. Ibid.
154. Irfan Habib, 'Marx's Perception of India', in Iqbal Husain (ed.) *Karl Marx. On India* (New Delhi: Tulika Books, 2006), p. XXXIV, n. 84
155. Karl Marx, 'The Eighteenth Brumaire of Louis Bonaparte', in *Marx Engels. Selected Works* (Moscow: Progress Publishers, 1975), p. 96.
156. Jotirao Phule, 'Slavery', in *Selected Writings of Jotirao Phule*, ed. G.P. Deshpande (Delhi: LeftWord, 2010), p. 50.
157. B.R. Ambedkar, 'Annihilation of Caste', in *The Essential Writings of B.R. Ambedkar*, ed. Valerian Rodrigues (New Delhi: Oxford University Press, 2008), pp. 264-7.
158. Ibid., p. 264.
159. Ibid., p. 265.
160. Ibid.
161. See his *The People of India* (London: Thacker, Spink and Co., 1908).
162. See Surinder Jodhka, *Caste* (New Delhi: Oxford University Press, 2012), p. 106.
163. Ibid., p. 158.
164. *In the Name of Marx*, p. 40.
165. B.R. Ambedkar, op. cit., p. 268.
166. Leon Trotsky, *The Permanent Revolution & Results and Prospects* (Delhi: Aakar Books: 2005), p. 40; Leon Trotsky, *The Revolution Betrayed* (Delhi: Aakar Books, 2006), pp. 102, 214, 256.
167. G.W.F. Hegel, 'On the Episode of the Mahabharata', in *Hegel's India. A Reinterpretation with Texts*, ed. Aakash Singh Rathore and Rima Mohapatra (New Delhi: Oxford University Press, 2017), p. 98.
168. Ibid., p. 99.

169. Ibid., p. 105.
170. Ibid., p. 110.
171. Ibid., p. 95.
172. B.R. Ambedkar, 'Annihilation of Caste', in *The Essential Writings of B.R. Ambedkar*, ed. Valerian Rodrigues (New Delhi: Oxford University Press, 2008), p. 267.
173. Ibid.
174. See his *Lokāyata. A Study in Ancient Indian Materialism* (New Delhi: People's Publishing House, 1992), *Carvaka/Lokāyata. An Anthology of Source Materials and Some Recent Studies* (New Delhi: Indian Council of Philosophical Research, 1994), *What is Living and What is Dead in Indian Philosophy* (New Delhi: People's Publishing House, 2010) and *Indian Philosophy. A Popular Introduction* (New Delhi: People's Publishing House, 1964).
175. *In the Name of Marx*, pp. 35-7.
176. Karl Marx, 'A Contribution to the Critique of Hegel's Philosophy of Right. Introduction', in *Karl Marx. Early Writings*, trans. Gregor Benton (New York: Vintage Books, 1975), p. 256.
177. Ibid., p. 256.
178. Ibid., p. 257.
179. Karl Marx, *Grundrisse*, trans. Martin Nicholas (London: Penguin Books, 1975), p. 471.
180. Ibid., p. 478.
181. Ibid.
182. Karl Marx and Frederick Engels, 'Manifesto of the Communist Party', in *Marx. Engels. Selected Works* (Moscow: Progress Publishers, 1975), p. 46.
183. Ibid.
184. Ibid., p. 45.
185. Lars Lih, *Lenin Reconsidered. What is to be Done? in Context* (Delhi: Aakar Books, 2013), p. 41.
186. Ibid., p. 43.
187. Ibid.
188. Karl Marx, 'Inaugural Address of the Working Men's International Association', in *Marx. Engels. Selected Works*, Volume Two (Moscow: Progress Publishers, 1977), p. 17.

189. Ibid., p. 18.
190. See Prabhu Bapu, *Hindu Mahasabha in Colonial North India, 1915-1930: Constructing Nation and History,* (London and New York: Routledge, 2013).
191. See Mark Tully, *Indian Express*, March 2, 2018.
192. B.R. Ambedkar, 'Struggle of Lowest Strata of Society is Bound to Help all Sections of Working Class', in *Dr. B.R. Ambedkar and His Egalitarian Revolution, Part III, Speeches. Dr. B.R. Ambedkar. Writings and Speeches*, Vol. 17, Part Three (Mumbai: Dr. Babasaheb Ambedkar Source Material Publication Committee, 2003), p. 239.
193. Ibid.
194. B.R. Ambedkar, 'Hindu Society Must Organize on Modern Lines Breaking Down Its Age-long Framework', in ibid., p. 220.
195. B.R. Ambedkar, 'Conversion is Necessary for Your Emancipation and Advancement', in ibid., pp. 107-112.
196. B.R. Ambedkar, 'What Way Emancipation?', in ibid., p. 145.
197. B.R. Ambedkar, 'My Philosophy of Life', in ibid., p. 503.
198. B.R. Ambedkar, 'What Congress and Gandhi Have Done to the Untouchables. Mr. Gandhi and the Emancipation of the Untouchables', in *Dr. B.R. Ambedkar. Writings and Speeches*, Vol. 9 (Mumbai: : Dr Babasaheb Ambedkar Source Material Publication Committee, 2016), p. 109.
199. M.K. Gandhi, *The Bhagavad Gita* (Mumbai: Jaico Publishing House, 2017), p. 107.
200. Ibid.
201. Ibid.
202. Ibid., p. 108.
203. Ibid.
204. Ibid., p. 7.
205. Ibid.
206. Ibid., p. 6.
207. Ibid.
208. Ibid.
209. Ibid., p. 10.
210. Ibid., p. 360.

211. See M.K. Gandhi, *Hind Swaraj or India Home Rule* (Ahmedabad: Navjivan Publishing House, 1998), p. 28.
212. Ibid., pp. 28-9.
213. Isaac Deutscher, *Stalin* (London: Pelican, 1965), pp. 343-6.
214. Ibid., p. 346.
215. Ibid.
216. N.S. Khrushchev, 'Speech Concerning the 'Cult of the Individual and its Consequences', 1956', in *The Stalin Question*, ed. Banbehari Chakrabarty (Calcutta: Kathashilpa, 1979), p. 9.
217. Erich Fromm, 'Trotsky's Diary in Exile-1935', in *Science & Society*, Vol. 66, No. 2, Summer, 2002, pp. 271-2.
218. Leon Trotsky, *The Revolution Betrayed* (Delhi: Aakar Books, 2006), p. 102.
219. Ibid., p. 103.
220. Joseph Hansen, op. cit., p. VII.
221. Leon Trotsky, op. cit., p. 214.
222. Ibid., p. 255.
223. Karl Marx, 'The Eighteenth Brumaire of Louis Bonaparte', in *Marx. Engels. Selected Works* (Moscow: Progress Publishers, 1975), p. 171.
224. Ibid.
225. Ibid., p. 168.
226. Ibid., p. 169.
227. Ibid.
228. Leon Trotsky, *The Revolutionary Betrayed*, pp. 61-4.
229. Ibid., p. 62.
230. Ibid., p. 63.
231. Karl Marx, 'Critique of the Gotha Programme', in *Marx. Engels. Selected Works* (Moscow: Progress Publishers, 1975), p. 320.
232. Leon Trotsky, op. cit., p. 65.
233. Ibid.
234. Ibid., p. 65.
235. Ibid., p. 61.
236. See D.D. Kosambi, *The Culture and Civilization of Ancient India in Historical Outline* (New Delhi: Vikas Publishing House, 2000), p. 50.

237. See Dilip Menon', 'Being a Brahmin the Marxist Way. E.M.S. Namboodiripad and the Pasts of Kerala', in *The Blindness of Insight. Essays on Caste in Modern India* (New Delhi: Navayana, 2011), pp. 32-72, especially p. 37.
238. Ibid., p. 35.
239. See Louis Althusser, *For Marx*, trans. Ben Brewster (London: Allen Lane, 1969), p. 209.
240. Karl Marx, *Capital*, Vol. I trans. Samuel Moore and Edward Aveling (Moscow: Progress Publishers, 1983), pp. 321-2
241. Ibid., pp 337-9.
242. Karl Marx, 'Despotism and the Enclosed State', in Lawrence Krader, ed., *The Asiatic Mode of Production. Sources, Development and Critique in the Writings of Karl Marx* (Assen: Van Gorcum & Comp. B.V., 1975), p. 75.
243. Ibid., p. 77.
244. Ibid.
245. Ibid., p. 76.
246. Ibid., p. 78.
247. Perry Anderson, *Lineages of the Absolutist State* (London: Verso, 1979), p. 466.
248. Karl Marx, 'Despotism and the Enclosed State', p. 76.
249. See Irfan Habib, *Essays in Indian History. Towards a Marxist Perception* (New Delhi: Tulika, 1997), pp. 180-232.
250. Ibid., p. 181.
251. See Karl Marx, 'Letter to the Editorial Board of the *Otechestevenniye Zapiski*', November 1877, in *Marx. Engels. Selected Correspondence* (Moscow: Progress Publishers, 1975), pp. 293-4.
252. Kevin Anderson, *Marx at the Margins*, pp. 52-6. Also see pp. 44, 50, 52, 138, 168 where Anderson mentions how Marx moves from his alleged "Eurocentric" view of the *Manifesto of the Communist Party* to more nuanced views on non-capitalist, non-Western societies.
253. Karl Marx, *Capital*, Vol. III (Moscow: Progress Publishers, 1986), p. 796.
254. Karl Marx, 'Despotism and the Enclosed State', p. 78.
255. Karl Marx, *Capital*, Vol. III, p. 791.
256. Karl Marx and Frederick Engels, , 'Preface to the Second Edition of the *Manifesto of the Communist Party*', in Theodor Shanin

(ed.), *Late Marx and the Russian Road. Marx and the Peripheries of Capitalism* (Delhi: Aakar Books, 2009), p. 139.

257. Frederick Engels, 'Principles of Communism', in *Marx. Engels. Collected Works*, Vol. 6 (Moscow: Progress Publishers, 1977).
258. Ibid.
259. Karl Marx, 'The Class Struggle in France', in *Marx. Engels. Selected Works in Three Volumes*, Volume One (Moscow: Progress Publishers, 1977), p. 213.
260. Karl Marx, 'The British Rule in India', in *Marx. Engels. On Colonialism*, p. 40.
261. Karl Marx, 'The Future Results of the British Rule in India', in ibid., p. 87.
262. Edward Said, *The Question of Palestine* (New York: Vintage Books, 1992), p. 3.
263. Kevin Anderson, *Marx and the Margins*, p. 165.
264. Ibid., p. 165; Karl Marx, *Capital*, Vol. III, trans. David Fernbach (London: Penguin, 1981), p. 732.
265. Ibid., *Marx. Engels. Collected Works*, Vol. 34, pp. 118-9.
266. Karl Marx, *Capital*, Vol. I, p. 29; Karl Marx, *Das Kapital*, Erster Band (Berlin: Dietz Verlag, 1981), p. 28.
267. Karl Marx, 'The British Rule in India', in *Marx. Engels. On Colonialism* (Moscow: Progress Publishers, 1976), p. 35.
268. Kevin Anderson, *Marx and the Margins*, p. 165; *Marx. Engels. Collected Works*, Vol. 34, pp. 118-9.
269. Karl Marx, 'The British Rule in India', p. 41.
270. See Marian Sawer, *Marxism and the Question of the Asiatic Mode of Production* (The Hague: Martinus Nijhoff, 1977), p. 159.
271. Shireen Moosvi, 'Sharing the 'Asiatic Mode'? India and Iran', in Irfan Habib (ed.), *A Shared Heritage. The Growth of Civilizations in India & Iran* (New Delhi: Tulika Books, 2002), pp. 177-188
272. Habib, 'Marx's Perception of India', p. XXXIV, n. 84.
273. Irfan Habib, *Essays in Indian History. Towards a Marxist Perception* (New Delhi: Tulika Books, 1995), p. 14; and 'Marx's Perception of India', in Iqbal Husain, edited *Karl Marx. On India* (New Delhi: Tulika Books, 2006), p. XVIX.
274. Irfan Habib, *Essays in Indian History. Towards a Marxist Perception*, pp. 35, 234.

275. Irfan Habib, 'Marx's Perception of India', p. XXVII, n. 46.
276. Ibid. XXVI.
277. Ibid. XX-XXII.
278. R.S. Sharma, *Early Medieval Indian Society. A Study of Feudalism* (Hyderabad: Orient Blackswan, 2013), pp. 45-76.
279. Kevin Anderson, op. cit., p. 163; *Marx. Engels. Collected Works*, Vol. 31, p. 276.
280. Ibid., p. 164; *Marx. Engels. Collected Works*, Vol. 34, p. 236.
281. William Dalrymple, *The Last Mughal. The Fall of Dynasty* (London: Penguin, 2007), p. 477.
282. Karl Marx, 'The British Rule in India', in *Marx. Engels. On Colonialism* (Moscow: Progress Publishers, 1976), pp. 40-41.
283. See my 'In Defence of Marxism: A Reply to a Neo-Hindu's Reading of *The Seductions of Karl Marx*', in *Critique*, Vol. 40, No. 1, February 20012, p. 109. See also my *The Legacy of Karl Marx* (Centre for Scientific Socialism: Nagarjuna University, 2012), pp. 56-7.
284. See Aijaz Ahmad, *In Theory. Classes, Nations, Literatures* (Delhi: Oxford University Press, 1994), p. 224.
285. Ibid.
286. Karl Marx, 'The British Rule in India', in *Marx. Engels. On Colonialism* (Moscow: Progress Publishers, 1976), p. 40; and Marx's 'Letter to Engels, June 14, 1853', in *Marx. Engels. Selected Correspondence* (Moscow: Progress Publishers, 1975), p. 80.
287. Karl Marx, 'The British Rule in India', p. 41.
288. Karl Marx, 'The Future Results of the British Rule in India', in *Marx. Engels. On Colonialism* (Moscow: Progress Publishers, 1976), p. 81.
289. Karl Marx, *Capital*, Vol. I, p. 20.
290. Karl Marx, *Economic and Philosophic Manuscripts of 1844* (Moscow: Progress Publishers, 1982), p. 91.
291. Kevin Anderson, op. cit., p. 165; *Marx. Engels. Collected Works*, Vol. 34, p. 118.
292. See *Rg Veda, Sacred Writings. Hinduism. Rg Veda*, trans. Ralf T.F. Griffith (New York: Quality Paperback Books, 1992), p. 603.
293. See Sigmund Freud, 'The Uncanny', in *The Penguin Freud Library. Vol. 14. Art And Literature*, translated under the general

editorship of James Strachey (London: Penguin Books, 1990), pp. 339-376.

294. See my *The New Militants* (Delhi: Aakar Books, 2014), p. 39 Also see Irfan Habib, 'Caste in Indian History', in *Essays in Indian History. Towards a Marxist Perception*, p. 169.
295. Irfan Habib, 'Caste in Indian History', p. 164.
296. Ibid., p. 169.
297. Ibid., p. 176.
298. Gherardo Gnoli, *Zoroaster's Time and Homeland. A Study on the Origins of Mazdeism and Related Problems* (Naples: Insitituto Universitario Orientale, 1980), p. 186.
299. B.R. Ambedkar, *Who Were the Shudras?* (Bombay: Thacker and Co. Ltd., 1970), pp. XIV-XV, XVII.
300. See Michael Bamshad, 'Genetic Evidence on the Origins of Indian Caste Populations', in *Genome Research*, 11 (6), June, 2001, https://www.ncbi.nlm.nih.gov/pmc/articles/PMC311057/.
301. Albêrûnî, *India. An Account of the Religion, Philosophy, Literature, Geography, Chronology, Laws and Astrology of India About AD 1030* (New Delhi: Rupa, 2002), p. 83.
302. See 'The Gathas of Zarathushtra', in *The Religion of Zarathushtra*, trans. I.J. S. Taraporewala (Bombay: B.I. Taraporewala, 1979), Y. 32.8, p. 155.
303. Shaul Shaked, 'First Man, First King', in *From Zoroastrian Iran to Islam* (Hampshire: Ashgate Publishers, 1995), p. 242.
304. See *Rg Veda*, Hymn X, 13.
305. *Pahlavi Vendidâd (Zand=I Jvît-Dêv=Dât)*, trans. B.T. Anklesaria (Mumbai: The K.R. Cama Oriental Institute, 2002), p. 16.
306. Shaul Shaked, op. cit., p. 244.
307. Firdausi, *Shâhnâma*, Vol. I, trans. George Warner and Edmund Warner (London: Kegan Paul, 1915), pp. 132-3.
308. Shaul Shaked, op. cit., p. 244.
309. See *Pahlavi Vendidâd*, pp. 16-38.
310. See Maurice Winternitz, *A History of Indian Literature*, Vol. I (New Delhi: Motilal Banarasidas, 1990), p. 60.
311. Ibid.
312. Ibid., p. 113.
313. Ibid., p. 184.

314. Partha Chatterjee, 'There is an Indian Ideology, But It's Not This', in *The Indian Ideology. Three Responses to Perry Anderson* (New Delhi: Permanent Black, 2015), p. 96.
315. See Kevin Anderson, *Marx at the Margins*, p. 167.
316. Ibid.
317. Ibid., p. 168.
318. Ibid., p. 155.
319. Frederick Engels, 'Feuerbach and the End of Classical German Philosophy', in *Marx. Engels. Selected Works*, pp. 589-90.
320. Ibid., p. 588.
321. Louis Althusser, *For Marx*, trans. Ben Brewster (London: Allen Lane, 1969), p. 230.
322. Ibid., pp. 29-30.
323. Karl Marx and Frederick Engels, *The Holy Family*, p. 116. See also my *Why We Are Not Hindus*, p. 57.
324. Karl Marx, *Economic and Philosophic Manuscripts of 1844*, pp. 127, 134, 143; Karl Marx, 'Nationalökonomie und Philosophie', in Karl Marx, *Die Frühschriften* (Berlin: Alfred Kroner Verlag, 1964), pp. 251, 271, 281.
325. Ibid., pp. 90, 91, 109, 132, 143; Ibid., pp. 236, 251, 264, 280-1, 282.
326. Ibid., pp. 90, 94, 109; Ibid., 264.
327. Ibid., p. 132; Ibid., p. 269.
328. Ibid., pp. 93-4; Ibid., p. 239.
329. Ibid., pp. 108-9.
330. Ibid., p. 143; Ibid., p. 281.
331. Ibid., p. 70.
332. Ibid., pp. 93-4; Ibid., p. 239.
333. Ibid., p. 98; Ibid., p. 245.
334. Ibid., 132; Ibid., p. 269.
335. Karl Marx, 'The Eighteenth Brumaire of Louis Bonaparte', p. 148.
336. Edward Said, *Orientalism* (London: Penguin, 1978), pp. 154, 206.
337. Harbans Mukhia, 'Was There Feudalism in Indian History?', in *The Journal of Peasant Studies*, Vol. 8, 198, Issue 3.
338. Kevin Anderson, 'Marx's Late Writings on Russia Re-examined', in *News & Letters*, November, (2007).

339. Karl Marx, 'First Draft of the Reply to V.I. Zasulich's Letter', in *Marx Engels. Selected Works*, Volume Three (Moscow; Progress Publishers, 1970), p. 152.
340. Ibid.
341. Ibid., p. 153.
342. Ibid., p. 152.
343. Karl Marx, 'Letter to the Editorial Board of *Otechestvenniye Zapiski*, London, Nov., 1877', in *Marx. Engels. Selected Correspondence* (Moscow: Progress Publishers, (1975), p. 293.
344. Ibid., p. 294.
345. Karl Marx, *Capital*, Vol. I, p. 20.
346. Karl Marx, 'The British Rule in India', in *Marx. Engels. On Colonialism* (Moscow: Progress Publishers, 1976), p. 40.
347. Irfan Habib, 'Caste in Indian History', in *Essays in Indian History. Towards a Marxist Perception*, p. 164.
348. Nicholas Dirks, *Castes of Mind. Colonialism and the Makings of Modern India* (New Jersey: Princeton University Press, 2001), p. 5.
349. Ibid., pp. 3-4.
350. Ibid., p. 7.
351. But then it would also challenge the readings of Megasthenes and Albêrûnî and surprisingly put them too in the cultural baggage of Orientalism.
352. Nicholas Dirks, *Castes of Mind. Colonialism and the Makings of Modern India*, p. 5.
353. Ibid., p. 12.
354. Ibid., p. 14.
355. Albêrûnî, op. cit., pp. 83-88.
356. Ibid., p. 83.
357. Nicholas Dirks, op. cit., p. 13.
358. Albêrûnî, op. cit., p. 87.
359. Nicholas Dirks, op. cit., p. 13.
360. B.R. Ambedkar, 'What Congress and Gandhi Have Done to the Untouchables', in *Dr. Babasaheb Ambedkar. Writings and Speeches*, Vol. 9 (Mumbai: Education Department, Government of Maharashtra, 2016), p. ii.

361. Karl Marx, *Economic and Philosophic Manuscripts of 1844*, p. 122.
362. Slavoj Žižek, 'Foreword to Trotsky. Terrorism and Communism, or, Despair and Utopia in the Turbulent Years of 1920', in *Slavoj Žižek Presents Trotsky. Terrorism and Communism* (London: Verso, 2007), p. XXXII.
363. Karl Marx, *Capital*, Vol. III, p. 817.
364. Ibid.
365. Karl Marx, *Capital*, Vol. I, p. 19.
366. Ibid.
367. Karl Marx, *Economic and Philosophic Manuscripts of 1844*, p. 132.
368. Karl Marx, *Capital*, Vol. I, p. 29.
369. Ibid.
370. Frederick Engels, 'Karl Marx', in *Marx. Engels. Selected Works* (Moscow: Progress Publishers, 1975), p. 372.
371. Quoted in Allen Bullock, *Hitler and Stalin. Parallel Lives* (London: HarperCollins, 1992), p. 394.
372. Theodor Adorno, *Prisms*, trans. Samuel and Shierry Weber (Cambridge, Massachusetts: The MIT Press, 1981), p. 34.